BON ECHO

The Denison Years

Mary Savigny

BON ECHO

The Denison Years

Mary Savigny

Natural Heritage Books

Published by Natural Heritage / Natural History Inc.
P.O. Box 95, Station O, Toronto, Ontario M4A 2M8

First Edition

ISBN 1-896219-30-6

Canadian Cataloguing in Publication Data
Savigny, Mary
  Bon Echo: The Denison Years
Includes index
ISBN 1-896219-30-6

Cover and text design by Steve Eby

Front cover painting by Arthur Lismer

Overleaf. Merrill Denison, Portrait by Nakash.

Back cover. Oil sketch of Mike's House by Mary Savigny

Inside front cover. Top, Nancy Palmer, Merrill and Yousuf Karsh on Dollywood Terrace, June, 1955. Middle, Merrill Denison by Openheimer (1964). Bottom, The aluminum painted inscription "Old Walt."

Inside back cover. Top, Plaque at the Playhouse, Tweed, Ontario. Bottom, In 1996 Merrill Denison's most serious drama "Marsh Hay" was fully premiered on the Shaw Festival Stage, more than seventy years following its original publicaton.

Quotations on inside covers from "*The Sunset of Bon Echo*" 1919 and 1916 editions.

Natural Heritage / Natural History Inc. acknowledge the support of the Canada Council for the Arts for our publishing program. We also acknowledge with gratitude the assistance of the Association for the Export of Canadian Books, Ottawa, and the Office of the Ontario Arts Council, Toronto.

The Canada Council | Le Conseil des Arts
for the Arts | du Canada
since 1957 | depuis 1957

Printed and bound in Canada by Hignell Printing, Winnipeg, Manitoba

Dedication

In memory of M.D.

Page from The Sunset of Bon Echo, April–May, 1920 issue. Caption reads Horace Traubel turning the Sod where the Corner Stone will be for The Whitman Library. Mrs. Bain, Mr. Penton, Mrs. Morris and Anne Montgomerie Traubel.

Page from The Sunset of Bon Echo, April–May, 1920 issue. Caption reads Horace Traubel and Flora MacDonald dedicating Canada's Gibraltar to the Democratic Ideals of Walt Whitman and naming it Old Walt. Mr. and Mrs. Morris and Mrs. Traubel also in the boat.

Contents

WALT WHITMAN

By Albert E. S. Smythe

Oannes, Lord of wisdom, time and toil,
   The Word in man, incarnate, evermore,
   Name above all, Amen, on Nilus' shore,
None other under heaven on Christian soil,
In India OM, from Whom the worlds uncoil,
   The Shepherd Krishna's Song, blind
      Homer's Lore,
   Gautama's Secret, and His Love who bore
The Cross, annointed King with David's oil:
These of the Elder Brethren dwelt on earth.
   And, God becoming man, raised Man
      to God—
     God-voices calling Peace from age to age.
And later came, through the strait gate of birth
   The World-Word, by sea-sand and
      prairie sod,
     With Leaves of Grass, simplicity most
      sage.

From *The Sunset of Bon Echo*, April-May, 1916 issue.

Foreword

GROWING UP IN ENGLAND, I learned very little about Canada. I knew it was a big, pink space on the world map. It was called the bread basket of the world and Grandma's sister had lived in a soddy in Saskatchewan. Typing Merrill Denison's manuscripts, I learned more about Canada than most who are born here. I learned something of the people who had created a nation in this immense and often formidable land which Merrill described as "a precarious creation, geographically, politically and racially."

Forty-odd years ago I learned something about publishing a book. Now I learn that I know nothing about publishing a book. Barry Penhale, whose eight years' of gentle persuasion brought me to write this, spoke of hard drive, hard disks, floppy disks, draft copy, hard copy and other strange concepts. I typed this manuscript as I always used to do, on a typewriter, of the sort now used as boat anchors.

My heartfelt thanks to my daughter-in-law, Karen, and my grandson, Michael, without whose patient help and up-to-date equipment at the office of Savigny Real Estate in Cloyne, I couldn't have coped. Loving thanks, too, to my three children; Janet Birnie, David and John Merrill, for their support and valuable contributions.

Alice and Frank Beswick deserve my thanks. They provided lots of information, not least of which are the early photographs of the Inn. The Beswicks were among the first to buy a Mazinaw property from Merrill and with their daughter, Jan Foy, became good friends of the Denisons.

Clyde Bell, who was editor and co-owner of *The Tweed News* from 1964 to 1986, responded instantly to my queries about his friendship with Merrill. He remembered hearing about the plays performed in the 1920's in the Orange Hall. He recounted that building's chequered history and eventual renovation to become The Tweed Playhouse. He told me, too, about Merrill's meeting with Aubrey Fessenden in 1930. Many thanks, Clyde.

The staff of the Archives of Queen's University, Kingston, were most helpful in guiding my husband and me to the right boxes in which to search for Bon Echo photographs.

It is to my best friend and husband of fifty-three years, John Savigny, I owe an enormous debt. When I was busy scribbling, he didn't complain about the dust bunnies assembling under the kitchen table. Without John's encouragement, patient cooperation and significant help all along the way this book would not have been published.

At Kingston, Ontario

MARY SAVIGNY 1997

ALL ROADS LEAD TO
BON ECHO

BON ECHO ROCK, MAZINAW LAKE, CLOYNE, ONTARIO

1950s postcard of Bon Echo Rock,
Mazinaw Lake, Cloyne, Ontario

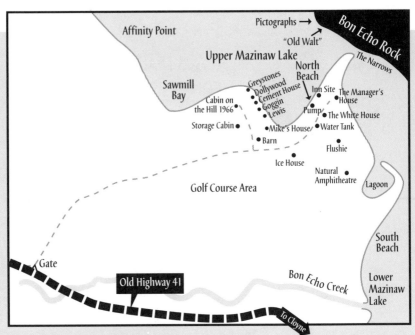

Bon Echo as it used to be.

Merrill, Lisa and Kelso Roberts admiring the plaque, 21st July, 1965.

Merrill cutting the ribbon, with J. R. Simmonett, Lisa and Kelso Roberts, 21st July, 1965.

Bon Echo as it is today.

Mike Schwager at his easel and author's oil sketch of Mike's House below.

Barry James Holloway.

Jane Hunter Holloway at her home in Arrow Rock, Missouri.

~ 1

Bon Echo from the Inside

ANY HUNDREDS OF PEOPLE visit and enjoy Bon Echo Provincial Park on Lake Mazinaw, near Cloyne, Ontario. Very few people know, or even care, about the man whose gift of land made their enjoyment possible. Merrill Denison was fifty-eight years old when my husband and I first met him in 1951. We could not have known how that meeting would eventually change the course of our lives. That meeting led to an association and friendship which lasted until Merrill died in 1975.

My husband, John Savigny, ex-RCAF, and I, a war bride and ex-WAAF, had given up what some people might have thought was a good life in Toronto, with a bright future. We had an apartment on Jarvis Street, John had an office job with Canadian Westinghouse, but it was hard to make ends meet and harder to see how we could ever own a home so, after a year in the city, we decided to leave it all behind. With help from the Department of Veterans' Affairs, we bought an old farmstead and three hundred acres on Highway 41, south of Northbrook, in Lennox & Addington County. The intention was to set up a radio repair and electrical appliance business.

On the 1st of August, 1947, with our two-year old daughter, Janet, and our two-month old Springer Spaniel, Sally, we loaded our possessions on our 1934 Chevrolet half-ton truck, said goodbye to the rat race and set off to face an unpredictable future in the wilds of Eastern Ontario. We also said goodbye to indoor plumbing, hot water on tap and heat at the flick of a switch. But we were free, able to direct our own destiny. Fortunately our wartime air force experiences in Britain had prepared us for less-than-luxurious living. That was helpful as our new home didn't even have a kitchen sink, but it did have electricity and out in the yard there was a well with a hand pump.

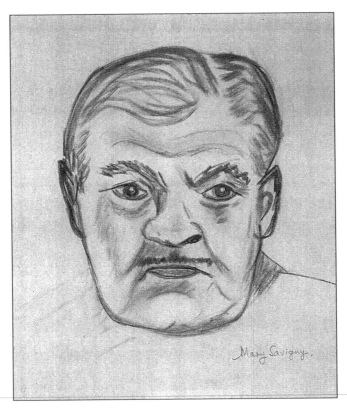

Author's sketch of Merrill Denison.

With John's wartime training and occupation in radar, further training in electronics and his interest in radio, he lost no time in setting up shop. With a few radio tubes, test equipment and tools, he was in business. On a tree beside the highway he hung a sign which I had painted. It proclaimed "Savigny Electric—Radio and Electrical Sales and Service." That very first day John had a customer who needed his radio repaired. The sun was shining, our little girl had a safe place to play, there were apples to be picked and we were happy.

It was over three years later that Mike Schwager, the caretaker at Bon Echo, brought in his battery radio. That being satisfactorily repaired, Mike came back to say that Mr. Denison would like John to go to Bon Echo, to repair his radio. During conversation at Bon Echo, Merrill asked John if he knew of anyone in the area who could type. John explained that I could, that I had typed manuscripts in England for Sir Osbert Sitwell and for his sister, Dame Edith Sitwell. "Beyond belief!" said Merrill and summoned John to bring me to Bon Echo.

Though it was a sunny afternoon in late summer when John drove me there, my first impression of Bon Echo was that it was a dark and gloomy place, with great pines keeping out the sun. I saw the Rock across the lake, a massive stone wall. In my English experience, holiday times were spent at the sea coast or on the Yorkshire or Derbyshire moors where the horizon was low and one could see forever. I wondered why anyone would want to spend their summers in such a confining place. The interview was conducted in the parking space between Greystones and Dollywood, the two largest cottages on the property. Merrill came out from Dollywood, a slow-moving man of medium height, somewhat overweight, with a large head and dark complexion. I sat in the car while Merrill, stern and unsmiling, peered in at me. The conversation has gone from my memory, but I'll always remember the penetrating stare of those deep brown eyes and two moles, one on each eyelid.

A few days later Merrill brought me the rough draft of an article about logging on the Ottawa River, I think it was. On my old Remington typewriter, circa 1924, I turned out the "fair copy," and those were the first of hundreds and hundreds of pages I typed for Merrill.

In those first years we had heard stories, myths and legends about Bon Echo. It was a vast, private estate in the north of Frontenac County with umpteen miles of shoreline on Lake Mazinaw, including the towering granite cliff known as Bon Echo Rock. Mr. and Mrs. Denison were summer people, a grumpy pair of authors who had no social connection with the village. No one dare set foot on the property. The gate at the highway was kept closed and, if spotted, anyone approaching by boat would be sent away. We were told that Bon Echo had been a summer resort, at one time run by Denison's mother who had had an inscription known as Old Walt carved on the face of the Rock. It was her tribute to an American poet, Walt Whitman, whose theories of world-wide democracy appealed to her.

Later, Denison's wife ran the place. Some could remember how strict and demanding she was. In 1936 the main building, Bon Echo Inn, burned and thereafter Bon Echo became the private summer retreat we came to know. We heard that naked little boys, painted like Indians, had been seen playing near the front gate. Merrill told us later that these were the children of W.O. (Bill) Mitchell, author of *Who Has Seen The Wind*. Their mother had used lipstick on their faces and tummies when they played Cowboys and Indians. It wasn't intended they should wander off as far as the gate.

A more serious criticism was that Denison had not only offended the local people, but he'd even made a lot of money from a book he had written which ridiculed the locals. That book was *Boobs In The Woods*, sixteen hilarious sketches of Muriel's and Merrill's unique experiences as managers of their wilderness summer resort. In no way was it a put-down of the local people. The "Boobs" were Muriel and Merrill. Of course, not one of those critics had actually read the book. It was all hearsay.

Michael Francis
Schwager, 1951.

Another story going around was that Denison owed several local businessmen a lot of money. That dated back to the collapse of the ill-fated company, Bon Echo Inn Limited, which proposed the building of a golf course and other expanded facilities at Bon Echo. The dream had faded with the 1929 stock market crash when the possibility of attracting well-heeled guests to the back-woods was slim indeed. The money owed by that company was not the Denisons' personal liability, but it was naturally assumed otherwise by the villagers.

Such local opinion led me to believe that I was becoming involved with, to say the least, some very difficult people. So it was with some trepidation that, in my best summer dress, I set off to hitch-hike the twenty-odd miles to Bon Echo to begin my sec-retarial duties. In those days traffic was light. The paved highway ended just north of Cloyne and became a gravel road, but I got a lift in a Sawyer-Stoll lumber truck which was going to the Massanoga Mill.

Mike Schwager met me outside his cottage and escorted me down the hill to Dollywood. It was large for a cottage, I thought, this box-like, two-storey, frame structure with clapboard siding. Mike took me to the back door beside which, unaccountably, was a milk delivery box and I noticed the numbers "1776" painted above the door. Merrill told me later that he'd painted the date there because he'd always wanted to live in a house dated 1776. While being guided through to the living room, I saw three French doors which opened onto the stone terrace. An enormous rough granite fireplace dominated the room. The curtains, braided rugs and cushions on the wicker chairs were blue. Merrill introduced me to his wife. I had pictured Mrs. Denison as an old-fashioned autocratic martinet, but I found her to be a charming lady even though she was suffering all the fearful symptoms of Parkinson's Disease. She made me feel quite at ease. Perhaps my English accent helped. As Merrill later said, she was "a profes-sional Royalist."

Merrill settled me into the room next to his. Bookshelves lined two walls and there were two tables. One was a long table under the window upon which stood an old black daffodil telephone, affording uncertain communication with the outside world. The other was a smaller one used as a desk. These tables, with birch legs, had been made on the property to furnish the Inn and all the various cottages. There were lots of them to be found in every building at Bon Echo. I knew the legs were birch because the bark was still on them.

Muriel's old portable Underwood typewriter was a disappointment to me. The moving parts didn't move very well and the type face was gummed up. I typed a couple of letters from Merrill's almost indecipherable handwriting and then found the courage to ask for an old brush, some lighter fluid and oil. Though he couldn't understand what I was going to do, he dutifully produced the tools. He was so intrigued with the process he said, "Let me try that!" Whereupon he sloshed lighter fluid over the type, brushed enthusiastically and splashed black ink on my best summer dress. He didn't notice. I didn't complain. Always I was to be amazed at his child-like curiosity and eagerness to learn about something new—even something so mundane as cleaning a typewriter.

Memories of those first years include the twice-weekly trips to Bon Echo. On one occasion a kindly trucker gave me a lift, but only to the gate, which was half a mile or so from the lakeshore where the cottages were situated. He said that if Mrs. Denison saw him she would "chase him off with a broom!" I later asked Merrill how this could be and he explained that years before, when the Inn was a going concern, the man had seduced one of Muriel's maids. Muriel had seen to it that he paid for his folly. For eighteen years he paid for the support of his child.

Though I found my own way to Bon Echo, Mike Schwager, the caretaker, brought me back in his Durant coupe or Merrill drove me home in Bundles, his 1940 Ford convertible. Muriel usually accompanied Merrill on these little jaunts. She insisted upon being suitably dressed, with her hair just so. But any movement was so difficult for her that, after we came to know each other, she asked me to help with such tasks as applying nail polish and hair combing. Muriel enjoyed seeing our children, Janet, then six, and David, two years old. David was special to her because he shared his name with her beloved father, the late Dr. David Goggin.

A trip home with Mike could be exciting. Coming downhill at speed around the S-bend of Devil's Elbow one day, Mike suddenly disappeared under the dashboard muttering something about "foot feed stuck agin!" He released the pedal and sat back up again just soon enough to keep the car on the road and me from having a premature heart attack.

A crusty old bachelor, Michael Francis Schwager, lived year round in his cottage at Bon Echo. He was a loyal employee and, in accordance with Mrs. Denison's strict orders, any curious trespassers promptly were sent packing. In the summer season his daily chores included a trip with his wheelbarrow to the icehouse to replenish the ice boxes in each cottage. The wood boxes had to be refilled. They were unusual in that, built into an external wall, they could be filled from outside. The bane of Mike's life was filling the coal oil lamps and cleaning the chimneys. He'd mutter and grumble the whole time, "By Jinjuss, you'd think these people would know how to light a lamp." "By Jinjuss" was Mike's frequently-used expression and the closest he ever got to swearing. He would trim the wick just so, yet despite his efforts some guest would turn it up too high, thus blackening the chimney.

Oil painting by Mike Schwager, c. 1950.

The winters at Bon Echo were long, cold and lonely. Often the road out to Highway 41 was blocked with snow. A welcome break came for Mike in November when a select few of his friends came in for the deer hunt. Another break in the monotony came when the crew came in to cut the ice. Mike's favourite solitary occupation was oil painting. He stood long hours at his easel where he painted countless impressions of the Big Rock in all the seasons, in rough weather and calm. Many of the Denisons' guests encouraged Mike and brought him art supplies.

The only other live-in employee was the cook-housekeeper who lived in the Cement House, where she prepared and served the meals. But of course she was only there for the summer. My memory of her is the mightily strong tea she served each afternoon and the watermelon which she unfailingly served as lunch time dessert.

Occasionally, Jean Hawley, who lived on the Pringle Lake Road, came to help with the cleaning. She was very deaf and wore a hearing aid, but she switched it off in order to save the battery. It was a severely frustrated Mrs. Denison who loudly called, "Hawley, Hawley, where are you?" and got no response. Merrill told me that, years previously, Hawley's husband, known as Arch, had been working at Bon Echo. Once after a long, hot day he washed his socks in the lake on the north beach, not very far from the pump house and the water intake. Mrs. Denison refused to drink the water for a week thereafter. Arch was not "Mister Clean," in fact his wife had become so disenchanted with him she sent him off to live in a shack by himself.

Completing the menage was the much-loved but undisciplined Irish terrier, Boo Boo, later to be known as Mister Boo. Merrill was too soft-hearted to even raise his voice to Mister Boo, consequently the little pooch did whatever he pleased. His greatest pleasure, it seemed, was riding in the convertible with Merrill. Whenever he heard the engine start he'd race from wherever he happened to be, eager and ready to go.

2
The Writer and His Wife

I N THAT YEAR OF 1951 Merrill was beginning work on the Molson saga, *The Barley And The Stream*. As he was later quoted as saying, he was not an author. He was a wordsmith, a craftsman, a fact-finder. His workmanlike method of assembling facts made accuracy a certainty. Many sheets of paper, about 20" by 36", ruled across and down, were used to list salient points.

Dates were listed in the boxes on the left, then came the name of the company chief of that year, then the names of people involved with the story and developments unfolding. Those sheets of paper were invaluable. Researchers and archivists provided a constant stream of information which Merrill correlated and entered on his data sheets.

Historical facts did not always find their way into print. Merrill told me that diligent research over many weeks suggested that John Molson Senior may not have married Sarah, the mother of his children. In his will Molson acknowledged their "natural children" as his beneficiaries. Merrill's account was a charming love story, a glimpse into the humanness of the characters involved, but it was never printed. Understandably, forty-six years ago, those members of the Molson family who had commissioned Merrill to write their business history did not wish such private details to become public. In the book Merrill refers to John Molson Senior as "young, self-willed and at outs with his guardian-grandfather."[1] He mentions Sarah and John's "life-long romance" which was "consummated" in 1786 and the birth of John Junior on the 14th October, 1787. The word "marriage" is not used.

Through the winters of 1951 to 1953 Merrill mailed his manuscript to me for typing from his New York apartment at 400 East 52nd Street. Soon he was working simultaneously on the Molson book and a history of the automotive industry, *The Power To Go*, for the Automobile Manufacturers' Association.

This was an American publication so American spelling was used. The Canadian story was written using the Oxford dictionary, with certain exceptions. It was then I asked Merrill why there wasn't a Canadian dictionary I could use. He wrote, "Now you're approaching the economics of Canadian publishing whose attenuated condition explains what some believe to be the lack of a Canadian culture. It would cost too much money!"[2]

For all the manuscripts I was required to produce as many copies as a ribbon and five. That meant winding six sheets of paper and five carbon sheets into the typewriter. With triple spacing, which left room for editing, I typed approximately two hundred words on each page. For each thousand words I received $1.30. Miss Conway Turton, McClelland and Stewart's editor, complained that the beer-coloured paper we were using for the Molson story was hard on the eyes. In a letter to me Merrill wrote, "Miss Turton says she would like white paper but that's a concession I shall never make."[3] And again he said, "We've already used pink, blue, canary and golden rod on the two books to date. It looks like green is the only thing left. Of course, there's always white to fall back on, but for some reason I have a prejudice against it."[4] The compromise was Grand and Toy's Eye-Saving Green, the paper we used thereafter.

As was right and proper, Miss Turton was a precise perfectionist. She and I exchanged several letters in ladylike argument about English usage and how to correctly type British pounds, shillings and pence. Finally I received a letter from her which said, "It was really rather silly of me to send you those further notes …don't let them bother you. What I meant to say before is that I have rarely seen such beautiful, even typing. Your work is certainly a pleasure to look at."[5] High praise indeed.

Muriel's condition continued to worsen and so Merrill was working under increasing pressure. Nevertheless, through it all, through frustrating revisions and re-writes, he remained cheerful, churning out chapter after chapter. His letters to me often included a touch of humour. For instance, when he mailed a Molson chapter he said, "…on getting into this phase of the story

I realized that Herbert Molson may well have been the angel from above who spared North America the ignomony (*sic*) of total prohibition. If the discovery can be documented the Molsons belong in the pantheon with Ben Franklin, Geo the Wash, Tom Jefferson, Andy Jackson, Abe Lincoln, Joe Demaggio (*sic*) and Marylin (*sic*) Monroe, and should be worth at least a bonus."[6]

In 1953 Merrill sublet the New York apartment from mid-May to the end of October, so that was a longer than usual stay at Bon Echo. It was to be Muriel's last. Again I hitch-hiked up there twice a week. Usually, I typed Merrill's letters, his manuscripts I typed at home. From time to time he produced a fistful of invoices and bills, invariably overdue. Mostly they were requests for membership fees from various authors' and historical associations, subscription notices from various magazines, insurance premiums and the dreaded $600-plus tax bills from Barrie Township for the more than 1,600 acres Merrill and Muriel owned. Though he had five bank accounts; two in New York, two in Toronto and one in Tweed, there was rarely enough on hand to cover the indebtedness. We juggled amounts to match the accounts and cheques were issued to satisfy the most urgent.

That Merrill, with blithe unconcern, would allow me to know how financially insecure he was, I found incredible. Most people thought he was wealthy. Obviously, at one time, he had earned enough to support himself and Muriel in the manner to which they had become accustomed. There were two establishments to maintain, each with whatever domestic help was necessary. Merrill's agent and researchers had to be rewarded. Muriel's medical bills were mounting. No expense was spared when she was taken to the finest doctors in the United States.

I was learning that money was not, and never had been, a priority in Merrill's life. However, by the late forties even he had seen that, regretfully, there was no alternative but to turn his talents to commissioned work. His pot boilers, as he called them, gave him a steady income, not always enough, but at least steady. He would much rather have been writing to satisfy himself, perhaps short comedies and radio plays. The Samuel French royalty cheques from his then best-known play, *Brothers-In-Arms*, brought a wry smile to his face. A high school production in Fort Churchill, Manitoba, would net him eight dollars.

Muriel Goggin Denison.

Unfortunately, the pot had to be kept boiling and Merrill's reputation as a corporate historian would come to overshadow his previous successes in light comedy, radio drama and plays. In 1948 McClelland and Stewart had published his *Harvest Triumphant*, the history of the Massey-Harris Company Limited and their contribution to Canada's manufacturing and agricultural development. The success of this book put Merrill's name on the very short list of Canada's corporate historians.

By then I was beginning to understand something of Merrill's complex character. He had a delightful sense of humour, with an even-tempered patience. He was a gentle man and I liked him. His first concern was for Muriel and that he loved her dearly was obvious. When I was there Muriel spent the afternoon in the Dollywood living room, resting on a recliner which Merrill had bought especially for her. It was a blue leather armchair with a foot rest and chromium frame which, incidentally, looked out of place in that woodsy atmosphere, but it travelled with her from New York to Bon Echo and back again. Eventually, Mike Schwager, in his old age, was able to enjoy it in his cottage.

Muriel frequently called for help. She needed to adjust her position, needed her book picked up from the floor, needed a fly swatted. Instantly, Merrill trotted off. Never was there the slightest indication that he lost his patience, never a sigh of frustration, never a muttered word of complaint, but always a loving response to her call. It amazed me that he could leave his typewriter in mid-sentence, attend to Muriel, then go right on typing as soon as he returned.

Later, during the winter of 1953-54, when Merrill mailed his manuscripts to me from New York, the yellow pages were handwritten. He explained that Muriel could no longer bear the noise of his typewriter. Such was Merrill's handwriting that, in my copy of *The Barley And The Stream*, he wrote, "For Mary Savigny, who suffered greatly also," and in the "Acknowledgments" he wrote, "To Mrs. Mary Savigny, who has typed the manuscript not once but three or four times, and from almost inscrutable copy, I extend my heart felt gratitude." [7]

Merrill and Muriel's love affair began soon after his mother, Flora MacDonald Denison, died in 1921. They met when they

Postcard c. 1930, The Inn, The Pump House, water tower upper right.

were both involved with the University of Toronto's Hart House Theatre where Merrill was the art director and set designer. I often wondered if Merrill, in finding Muriel and their love for each other, realized how fortunate he was? This was a well-educated lady who moved in the best society in Canada and England, Muriel was the daughter of a distinguished Canadian educator, Dr. David Goggin, who had been Superintendent of Education in the North-West Territories, Principal of the Manitoba Normal School and Chancellor of Trinity College, University of Toronto. She had lived in London, England, to further her singing career, but in 1916 when at last prepared for the concert stage, she became ill with acute appendicitis. After a long convalescence with Goggin relatives in Ireland she returned to Toronto, never to sing professionally.

But music was not her only interest. While in London she became interested in the management of large households, cookery and the manner in which servants should present food at table. I would never have believed this, but later Merrill gave me her cookery books and a notebook wherein she copied recipes.

BON ECHO INN
DAILY REPORT
August 10 th 1922. 19

No. of guests last 24 hours........	52			
No. out	1			
No. expected	0			
MEALS SERVED—				
Guests	156			
Kitchen	47			
Ex. Staff	15			
			218.	
House value per day			180.25	
COSTS—				
Staff meals (per meal)	23	10.21		
Guest meals (per meal)	28	47.88		
Wages (per day)		27.30	85.99	
RECEIPTS—				
Board		104 00		
Counter		12 35		
Boats				
Trans.		1.50		
Total			117.85	
Bus			8.00	
EXPENSES—				
Wages due		374.00		
Bills payable		1210.44	1584.44	
Bank Balance		130.05		
Cash in Hand		717.85		
Accrued House Value		681.30	1529. 20	

....
.... Prop.
....
.... Mgr.

Bon Echo Inn Daily Report, August 10, 1922.

Using a broad J nib and black ink, a writing style often favoured by English ladies of her day, Muriel listed ingredients for cakes and puddings. She noted the meals served at luncheon and dinner parties she attended, with drawings showing how the table was set and how each course was served. There are notes about how one should direct one's servants.

Her London address, inscribed on the first page, was 30 Dorset Square, Regents Park, N.W., certainly a fashionable address. One of her friends was a Miss Coutts, a daughter of the famous London banking family. It might have been that Muriel, having spent her younger days with her father in the rough and ready Canadian west, felt the need to learn how the more genteel households were run. Perhaps she envisioned life as the chatelaine of an English country house.

In any event, her life changed when she met Merrill. Without delay he took her to Bon Echo. This Irish redhead, with temperament to match, used her considerable talents to help Merrill manage Bon Echo Inn. With no electricity, light was provided by countless coal oil lamps. Food was kept cool in ice boxes and wood stoves were used for cooking and heating. However, Muriel's childhood experiences on the Prairies would have been some preparation for her new life.

Muriel's first working summer at Bon Echo was 1922, presumably as Merrill's employee. She was in charge of food purchasing, preparation and service. As Merrill soon realized her competence, she found herself in charge of the whole operation. Truth be told, Merrill would much rather pursue his writing career than run a business. Muriel used her London notebook again, now making hurried entries in pencil, such as noting, "Buying 1 Jersey, 1 Ayrshire—wild, Holstein—black and white." One can but guess as to why the Ayrshire was wild. Without doubt the Holstein was black and white and thus easy to identify. There are detailed instructions for washing a cream separator, washing cows' udders before milking and one alarming entry, "How to wash clothes clean. One tub water. One cup gasoline."

Whereas her mother-in-law had run the Inn as a summer camp, serving simple meals and employing few servants, Muriel's ambition was to create a luxury resort catering to a much wealthier clientele. With serious determination, "Fiery Nell," as Merrill called her in *Boobs In The Woods*, devoted herself to ensuring that the business prospered. She hired and trained various members of the staff. It has been said, and I'm sure it's true, that she hired up to twelve Scottish girls through an employment agency and taught them to serve in the dining room. They wore uniform which had to be clean and neat. Muriel lined them up for inspection before they went on duty. Much later, in 1954, when I was taking on the management of Bon Echo and Muriel was only weeks away from death, Merrill told me she had somehow got herself out of their New York apartment and he found her waiting for the elevator.

Asked what she was doing, she replied that she had to get to the employment agency to be sure that Mary would have the twelve Scottish maids she was surely going to need.

There were almost as many staff as there were guests at the Inn. Sometimes more. There were men to look after the wood supply, men to look after the boats for the guests, kitchen maids, cleaning maids and several Chinese who looked after the laundry. Merrill told me the story of one unfortunate Chinese laundryman who, on an evening off, ventured onto the upper lake in a canoe and was drowned in the three hundred and fifty feet depth in front of the Rock.

Long before the guests arrived there was work to be done. In February, ice from the lake was cut and stored. Later the vegetable and flower seeds were planted. Boats were repaired and painted, wood was cut and piled and winter's debris was swept away. At the end of the season there was still more work. Muriel had a system. All the bed mattresses were wrapped around with newspaper because mice won't chew through printer's ink. The mirrors were placed face down on the beds to hold the newspaper in place. So that mice wouldn't get into the pillows they were suspended, by sewn-on tapes, on coat hangers hooked to the ceiling. Every window pane, and there were hundreds in dozens of casement windows, was coated with Bon Ami, not polished off, but left so that intruders could not see inside. Big closets in Dollywood and Greystones were lined with tin so that all the blankets, linens, curtains, mats and carpets were safe from mice. I presume there were similar closets in the Inn.

Muriel's favourite colours for Bon Echo, Merrill told me, were blue and gold; the blue of the lake and sky and the gold on the Rock at sunset. Some curtains were of blue cotton, some of orange cotton, tablecloths were blue and white, with napkins to match. Phoenix Bird was the pattern of the blue and white crockery, then inexpensive but impressive. It was imported, wrapped in straw and packed in barrels, from Japan. The breakfast dishes were a speckled golden-orange and all was in harmony, from egg cup to demitasse.

The Denisons were not reticent when it came to advertising. Their colourful brochures, with many photographs and sketches, would have done justice to the Banff Springs Hotel. Prose in praise of the Inn is Merrill Denison at his fulsome best.

"BON ECHO INN is located on the point of land dividing the Upper and Lower Mazinaw Lakes. Its verandahs command views of the lake and hills for miles in both directions. Opposite the Inn is the Big Rock of Bon Echo. This Canadian Gibralter, a mighty mass of red granite, rises sheer out of the lake to a height of over 400 feet and is over a mile and a half in length. It is impossible to describe the magnificence of this scene when the great cliff is bathed in the rays of the setting sun, or to catch with words something of its serene majesty under a full moon. The Big Rock is as striking a natural prospect as the Capes of the Saguenay or the Ramparts of Quebec. MEALS. The food is such as one would expect to find in the home of an imaginative and accomplished hostess rather than at a summer inn. They are planned and prepared under the direct supervision of the Manager, whose staff in this department includes experts found only in the largest and most elaborate hotels. Bon Echo's picnic baskets are delectable surprises. An abundance of cream and milk is supplied from our own herd, and vegetables from gardens operated for exclusive use. CHILDREN. Working on lines approved by one of Canada's leading children's specialists, Bon Echo is unique among Canadian resorts in making a speciality of children's diet. On arrival, mothers or nurses are requested to fill out a comprehensive feeding chart, showing prohibited foods, special methods of food preparation, etc. This is followed by The Diet Kitchen. The smaller children have their meals in a separate dining room under the supervision of expert dietitians. The two shallow bathing beaches of white sand, and the quietness of the separate cottages, etc., makes Bon Echo particularly desirable for children."[8]

THE BIG ROCK AT BON ECHO

BON ECHO INN

BonEchoInn
On the Mazinawe Lakes
via CANADIAN PACIFIC RY. to
KALADAR, ONT.
GOOD FISHING, BOATING & OTHER OUTDOOR SPORTS

Various illustrations, done in the 1920s, of the Big Rock at Bon Echo. Top left, a sketch by Frank (Franz) Johnston for the Bon Echo Inn Brochure. Above, Franklin Carmichael's cover for an advertising brochure and left, a poster painted by A.Y. Jackson.

ONE ROOM BUNGALOW

RATES

Bon Echo operates on daylight saving time.

Rates—$5.00 to $8.00 per day.

INN—from $21.00 per week per person, with two persons in a room; up to $49.00 per week per person, with one person in a room.

ONE-ROOM LOG BUNGALOWS—$70.00 to $80.00 per week, for two persons; for three persons $90.00 per week.

TENTS—Wood floors, flys, two single cot beds, dressing stand, etc., two persons, $48.00 to $56.00 per week. One person, $28.00 to $31.50 per week.

COTTAGES—Rates for cottages will be quoted on application. The cottages have two, three, four, five and eight rooms.

The above rates include meals.

CHILDREN—Where children occupy accommodation with their parents half rates will be charged; where they occupy separate accommodation, full rates.

BOATS—Row boats and canoes; $1.50 per day; $6.00 and $7.00 per week. Outboard motor boats; $5.00 per day; $25.00 per week.

Bon Echo Inn, Limited,　-　Bon Echo, Ontario
Telegraph Address　- - - - Kaladar, Ontario
Telephone via　- - - - - - Tweed, Ontario
Prior to June 15th, 91 St. Joseph St., Toront

THE WATER'S FINE

Images of a gentler time when guests of Bon Echo Inn could relax in a "Vacation Estate in the Woods" as this early brochure describes. Guests enjoyed "amusements and interests both for those who seek rest and recreation, and those who want their holiday teeming with activity." These images portray the tranquillity and comfort of a Bon Echo vacation.

ONE OF THE COTTAGES

THE INN

A COTTAGE LIVING ROOM

A BUNGALOW INTERIOR

Prospective guests were assured that "Hay Fever is unknown at Bon Echo. Sufferers from this disease find immediate relief upon arrival, and complete immunity in a short time." All this was available, for two persons in a room, for from $56 to $70 per week.

This brochure continues to describe the wonders of Bon Echo, such as the Little Theatre where, two or three times during the week, guests and staff produced "rollicking plays written on the place and about the place."[9]

In the early 1970's Merrill was researching files at *The Tweed News* office and he told the editor, Clyde Bell, that some of those "rollicking plays" had been performed in Tweed in the 1920's. For two or three years, at the end of the season, the Bon Echo Thespians performed at the Orange Hall which had, Merrill said,

THE THEATRE

A production is in full force in The Little Theatre, above. Right, a portrait of Merrill in theatrical costume, tempra on card by Frank (Franz) Johnston.

the best stage north of Belleville. It was a two-day trip for the group when they set off from Bon Echo and bumped down to Kaladar in Merrill's McLaughlin Buick. The group would have included friends from the Hart House Theatre. The morning train took them to Tweed. After checking into the hotel, they set up the stage and rehearsed in the Orange Hall. Merrill's play *The Weather Breeder*, was first performed there.

For some of the plays the cast had only handwritten scripts from which to learn their lines. Seats for the evening performance of the one-act play cost 50 cents for adults, 25 cents for children, those under five got in free and standing room only cost 10 cents. Proceeds were donated to the local church choir. The ladies of the church provided supper. The next morning Merrill and his group packed up and then caught the train back to Kaladar. During the ride back to Bon Echo in the McLaughlin Buick, Merrill told Clyde Bell, they all sang. "It helped take our minds off the damn bumps."

From 1922 to 1929 guests were welcomed at Bon Echo. Many had well-known names. Included among them were several Group of Seven members. Arthur Lismer, a particular friend of Merrill's, was there quite often. Frank Carmichael, A.Y. Jackson and Frank Johnston were there also. They were all old friends from Hart House days. Merrill was amused by Frank Johnston's insistence that he now be known as Franz, less plebeian! Of course, they were all inspired by the Rock. Franz produced sketches which were used in the advertising brochures. Alex Jackson climbed the Rock and produced a small oil painting showing the narrows and the lagoon on the lower lake. This painting was in Merrill's possession until the late sixties when, as it often did, the need for cash arose. A Montreal dealer, a friendly neighbour of Merrill's, paid $2,900 for it on a Saturday evening and she gleefully told me she sold it on the following Wednesday for $3,500. In 1924 Jackson designed the Bon Echo poster. It reads, "Bon Echo Inn on the Mazinawe (sic) Lakes, via Canadian Pacific Ry. to Kaladar, Ont. Good fishing, boating and other outdoor sports." In 1928 Frank Carmichael designed a particularly dramatic cover for the Inn's brochure.

By 1926, the year Muriel and Merrill were married, the colonization road north of Cloyne had been improved and the Inn's brochure advises that "The Bon Echo Motors meets trains daily except Sunday at Kaladar Station." An added attraction was to be a nine-hole golf course "... designed by Stanley Thompson, Canada's leading golf architect. It is expected to be one of the smartest resort courses in the Province when completed." Those were brave words. The golf course was never completed. It was becoming clear to Muriel and Merrill that their business, now Bon Echo Inn Limited, could not achieve the success they had envisioned. It would be surprising if any commercial enterprise with such heavy operating expense could be successful when it was in operation only from June 30 to September 11. In 1929 the company declared bankruptcy and the Inn closed.

A glimmer of hope shone in the person of the Ontario Deputy Minister of Lands and Forests. He was William Finlayson who, with his wife, had been a guest at the Inn. He had become Merrill's friend and would remain so throughout the years. Their mutual interest in land use and conservation led to the suggestion that Bon Echo become a "Bush University." Unfortunately, that hope faded when a forestry school was set up instead at Dorset.

Merrill had continued writing while Muriel had gallantly borne the burden of the day-to-day operation of the Inn. He became a regular contributor to *The Toronto Star Weekly*, alternating between humourous essays about life in the backwoods to critical comment about the same area where wealthy lumber barons had cut down the forest, leaving a poverty-stricken population to eke out a living from the denuded land. Too poor and under-educated to seek employment elsewhere, they lived out their joyless lives in what Merrill termed "a rural slum."

3

Keeping the Wolf from the Door

INCE HIS RETIREMENT, Muriel's father, Dr. Goggin, had lived with the Denisons. At Bon Echo he occupied a one-room log cabin near the beach, next to the Cement House. At the end of September, 1929, leaving only a caretaker in charge at Bon Echo, the three returned to their Toronto home at 91 St. Joseph Street, to contemplate the future. In October the stock market collapsed. With very little financial gain, Merrill was still writing for *The Star Weekly*, in cooperation with Greg Clark and Jimmie Frise, sometimes with Ernest Hemingway and Walter Bowles. But the U.S. beckoned.

In a short time Merrill was in New York City, leaving Muriel and her father in Toronto. Some of the letters they exchanged still remain. Muriel, like most wives, was anxious that her husband project a good image. She reminded him to wash his chamois gloves. He replied that he had, he'd worn them last night when he took a bath. They missed each other very much. An undated letter reads:—

"Sunday AM

Dearest Mrs. Love,

It's late but I want to save you from an empty tin box and besides I'm very much in love—with you. I'm just in from shamelessly enjoying myself at the Bates. I went at 3.00 and left at 12.30. Perhaps it is unnecessary to say that I liked them very much. I humbly ask forgiveness for disgracing myself by such a long stay, but it's damn seldom that one meets human beings down here that when the occasion does happen it must be embraced.

All my love, dear woman, and an especially significant kiss good night for this is the 23rd.

Merrill"

Eventually, by knocking on the right doors, success was his. For NBC he wrote radio drama. He told me that he authoured the first radio soap opera, *Jack and Jill*. It was at NBC that Merrill met Barry Holloway. He was one of their publicity men and the two became instant friends. Over the years the Denisons and the Holloways spent much time together. Years later, Barry and his wife, Jane, became our friends too.

Although Muriel adored the man, she had very serious misgivings about Merrill's consistently flippant attitude toward their

Barry Holloway, Muriel Denison and Merrill Denison, c. 1945.

family finances. While he was in New York she vented her anger by writing the following in her account book:—

"I cannot keep accurate books unless my accounts and Bank account are left alone. In some way that I have not sufficient training to show, my accounts from April 7th to May 7th, have had taken from them by Merrill,

(1) an unknown sum which was given to the Bankrupt estate.

(2) my May to June allowance from Father had an amount taken from it. Again, I cannot show what this amount is, for Merrill filled in the signed cheques and later made up the statement and entered it in this book, in a way that I cannot understand.

I am of the opinion that the balance of my account of $520.00 to be used from April 7th to May 7th, 1930, was drawn by Merrill for the estate. Further, on or about April 24th he drew my May 7th to June 7th allowance from Father and deposited it in my account.

(1) My belief is that Merrill drew the balance of my account on or about April 24th for the estate. This left no money for outstanding cheques—or in other words an overdraft.

(2) Merrill got my May 7th to June 7th allowance from Father and put it in my account. Against this there were outstanding cheques from April 7th to May 7th, or an overdraft.

(3) The remaining cash disbursements belonging to April 7th to May 7th drawn by me necessitated cash withdrawals on the May 7th to June 7th allowance for April 7th to May 7th disbursements. I would appear to have had cash taken from my April 7th to May 7th allowance and from my May 7th to June 7th allowance.

When I agreed to borrow $2,000 from the Bank of Commerce and secured the collateral, it was on the promise of Merrill that he would meet the B. Echo caretaker's wages, insurance and taxes until July 15th 1931, without scenes, grumbling or recriminations, for this money was borrowed only to keep him from going into Court with the Creditors, thus wasting time he wanted to devote to his career.

This money was arranged for before Merrill returned to town, but not borrowed until he returned and expressed his consent and satisfaction with the arrangement. From April 7th to May 7th I had to sell my remaining bonds and paid $80.00 to Holmsted & Sutton for interest on the B.E. mortgage, one half of which Merrill had agreed to pay and did not. $250.00 to Holmsted & Sutton on their account, $60.00 wages to Sam Armstrong, $19.00 for motorcar repairs.

Muriel Denison. May 31st, 1930."

By way of explanation it should be noted that Dr. Goggin, Muriel's father, paid $120.00 each month as house allowance. Holmsted & Sutton were the Denisons' Toronto solicitors. Sam Armstrong was then the caretaker at Bon Echo and he was supposed to receive $60.00 monthly.

Fortunately, Merrill's star was rising and he was thoroughly enjoying his pioneering work as the writer of plays meant particularly for radio. There were challenges to be met in the broadcasting studio. Sound effects were a necessary feature of a play and taxed the ingenuity of the staff. The carbon granule directional microphones, adequate for one voice, necessitated the players stepping to the mike, in turn, to read their lines, being careful not to rattle their scripts.

Those first broadcasts caught the attention of an old man in Bermuda, called Reginald Aubrey Fessenden. In New York City, in 1930, he met with Merrill to talk about microphones. Merrill knew nothing about wireless transmission. He didn't own a radio. His job was to write the radio plays. Over a long lunch, using many sheets of paper, Aubrey Fessenden drew diagrams and explained non-directional microphones to Merrill. This conversation led to improvements at NBC and CBS.

Though Marconi had transmitted a spark-induced wireless signal from Cornwall, England, to St. John's, Newfoundland, in 1901, Merrill was convinced that it was the Canadian-born physicist and

THE TORONTO STAR WEEKLY, SATURDAY, MARCH 15, 1930

A PAGE ABOUT PEOPLE

~ *Sidelights on Men and Women in the Public Eye* ~

Merrill Denison

A portrait of Merrill Denison by Grant Macdonald.

engineer, R.Aubrey Fessenden, who really was the father of modern radio broadcasting. On the 14th December, 1906, he had broadcast his voice and played Handel's "Largo" on the violin from Brant Rock, Massachusetts, and astonished sailors manning Fessenden radio receivers on United Fruit Company ships and U.S. naval vessels in the Atlantic and as far away as the West Indies.

Merrill went on to an assignment with the Canadian National Railway, which then operated the radio broadcasting system in Canada. In 1931 Station CNRM, Montreal, broadcast over a chain of thirteen Canadian National and three associated stations. Eventually, the system became the Canadian Broadcasting Corporation. Merrill wrote *The Romance Of Canada*, a series of radio plays which brought some of Canada's history into the living rooms of those people lucky enough to own a radio receiver. With the skill he demonstrated in all his writing, Merrill brought to life a few of the personalities who had made Canada a nation. They included Alexander Mackenzie, Pierre Radisson, Henry Hudson, Laura Secord, James Wolfe and The Marquis de Montcalm.

In 1932, Muriel was able to join Merrill in New York. In closing their Toronto home many of their possessions were put in storage, there to remain until 1954, by which time the storage fees far exceeded the value of the stored items. Although she was not as compulsive and persistent a writer as Merrill, she had, over the years, been writing articles for such magazines as *Reader's Digest* and *McCall's*. Once settled with Merrill and her father in their West 57th Street apartment, Muriel began writing a successful series of books for young girls, beginning with *Susannah: A Little Girl With The Mounties* for Dodd, Mead & Company. In many respects this was autobiographical and so made an entertaining and believable story.

Born in Winnipeg, she had spent her early years with her father in Regina, then the capital of the North-West Territories. The book jacket blurb explains that "she spent much of her time in the Barracks of the North-West Mounted Police, rode the Canadian prairies with her red-coated friends, who were her wise counsellors, beloved teachers and good companions."

The success of this book led to a film contract with Twentieth Century Fox. Shirley Temple starred as Susannah and the movie was a hit. In spite of Merrill's initial scepticism, Muriel had made a name for herself as a writer of books for juveniles. She went on to write more of the same, *Susannah Of The Yukon*, *Susannah At Boarding School* and *Susannah Rides Again*. Her final book was another success. It was *Happy Tramp*, a story about a little girl and her sheepdog.

Each year the Denisons spent their summers at Bon Echo, living and working in Dollywood, taking their meals in the Cement House and accommodating occasional guests in Greystones. The Inn stood empty, but Merrill continued to investigate any possibility of developing the whole property. Any thought of dividing the shoreline into cottage lots was an anathema to him, not to be contemplated under any circumstances. Hope ran high when the Canadian Pacific Railway showed considerable interest, only to

David and Jane Holloway, 1954.

be dashed when it was decided to build what later became the Seignory Club in Quèbec.

A modest but much more practical scheme to offset some of the expenses was renting the Inn, the White House and the Manager's House as a boys' camp. Following that venture, three brothers from Belleville, Clair, Walter and Arthur Leavens, who were then in aviation and later boat building, re-opened the Inn. It was during their tenure, on September 16, 1936, that the Inn burned. Struck by lightning during a severe thunderstorm, the wooden structure, decorated with birch bark on columns, staircase, bedsteads and tables, burned to the ground in a short time. Fortunately no one was badly injured, but the two remaining guests and the staff lost all their clothing and personal possessions. The estimated loss was $25,000, only partly covered by Merrill's insurance.

In the ensuing years the Denisons followed their set pattern of winters in the city and summers at Bon Echo. Driving north from New York, their routine was to break the journey at Perth to stay a couple of days with their old friends, Winnie and Cyril Inderwick, who lived in the beautiful old house, "Inge-Va," on Craig Street. It is famous as the site of the last duel fought in Canada and now is one of Perth's tourist attractions. Cyril, so Merrill said, had been the inspiration in 1921 for his one-act play, *Brothers-In-Arms* and was Major J. Altrus Browne of the Army Service Corps, one of the four characters in the play.

Merrill, of course, was still writing. A book which became a best-seller and Book-of-the-Month Club choice, was *Klondike Mike*. Subtitled *An Alaskan Odyssey*, it was the life story of Mike Mahoney, a Canadian hero of innumerable Klondike gold rush legends. Perhaps the best-remembered is the one about Mahoney carrying a piano over the Chilkoot Pass into Dawson City just to accommodate six female entertainers.

Sadly, by 1942, Muriel was becoming ill and doctors at the Mayo Clinic diagnosed Parkinson's Disease. Among their many friends, it was Jane and Barry Holloway who gave unfailing support throughout Muriel's long illness. Then living in New Rochelle, they stayed with Muriel in New York when it was necessary for Merrill to travel to Detroit, Montreal or Toronto to consult with his publishers, as well as helping in many other practical ways. Both Jane and Barry were Southerners from Missouri, a delightful, generous and happy pair. With their son, Hunter, they were often at Bon Echo.

My husband, John, and I met them in the summer of 1953. We all enjoyed fishing, but perhaps Barry was the least dedicated. One evening, in the moonlight near the narrows, Barry was becoming a tad impatient. He lit a cigarette, reeled in his luminous mouse, his favourite lure, and jigged it up and down right beside the boat. To everyone's utter astonishment, a smallmouth bass leapt to his lure. It was the only fish caught that evening. Our laughter and the noise we made sent other fish far away.

Though Merrill owned a handsome fishing rod, he never used it, to my knowledge, though he loaned it to others. He was not interested in fishing, hunting or even bird watching. He once told me he had been given a BB gun when he was a youngster. Taking aim at a robin it fell to the ground and Merrill realized he had killed for no good reason. Never again would he hold a gun with intent to kill. One would suppose that his main interest in owning Bon Echo would have been the opportunities to hunt, fish and ramble over the countryside. But not so. Upon arrival at Bon Echo, usually in May, he would park the car between Dollywood and Greystones. Mike would be on hand to greet them, assist Muriel and unpack the luggage. Merrill would stand for a few minutes gazing at the Rock in silent communion then retreat into Dollywood, there to pour himself a finger or so of rye and a splash of Mazinaw water. He didn't even go for walks. As he often said, he despised walking as a means of locomotion.

During the winter of 1953-54 Muriel became house-bound. It seemed she would never be able to go to Bon Echo again. It was then that Barry Holloway had a flash of inspiration. He suggested to the Denisons that the Savignys might be interested in running Bon Echo as a housekeeping resort. Such an arrangement might help with the expenses. Our priority, of course, was Savigny Electric, which John still ran from our home, but the prospect of some extra income for us was attractive. It was agreed that I should take on the responsibility of taking inventory to begin with, then cleaning and preparing the cottages, advertising and generally taking charge.

The only person who was less than enthusiastic was Mike

Left, Janet, Mary and David
with Gazebo in background.
Below, Carol Brown, John,
Janet, David and Mary, 1954.
Bottom, The Savignys, John,
Mary, Janet and David,
outside the White House.
Note Bon Ami on Window.
Early, 1954.

Schwager, the caretaker. He had been Bon Echo's major domo since 1939. He was a well-known character in the area and enjoyed his status as the Denisons' representative. Years previously, he liked to relate, he had been the chief carpenter when Skootamatta Lodge was built for the Pearson family in the 1920's. A rambling conglomeration of granite and log, it rivalled Bon Echo Inn in size and splendor. In those days, Mike had lived on a wee island in Skootamatta Lake, where there was just enough space for his cabin and the outhouse. He was heart-broken when the love of his life wouldn't marry him because she refused to live with him on his little island.

At Bon Echo he had thoroughly enjoyed entertaining the Girl Guide troops who, with the Denisons' permission, camped for several summers in the area of the White House. But this scheme of the Savignys, "by Jinjuss," was a whole new ball game. The thought of all the cottages being filled with strangers was not to be borne. The thought of being at their beck and call, having to carry firewood, ice and coal oil to them was beyond contemplation. Think of all those blackened chimneys! Mrs. Denison, he claimed, was not going to agree to this harebrained scheme.

It was necessary for Merrill to write to Mike explaining the plan; that in his absence the Savignys would be taking charge and asking for his cooperation. Money earned from renting the cottages would ensure that Mike's wages were paid more frequently. Since 1936, when the Inn burned, Merrill estimated that taxes, insurance, caretaker's wages, ice cutting and storage had cost him over $2,000 a year for a total of $35,000, therefore any help I could give would be welcome, he said. Mike accepted his fate, sometimes with good grace, sometimes not.

The inventory uncovered some discrepancies. For instance, there were 186 huckaback hand towels and only 14 tea towels. It was the Denisons' custom to pack the whole season's laundry into a big wooden box and ship it by rail to the Brighten Laundry in Toronto. Enquiry addressed to the Brighten Laundry revealed that the box had been received at Kaladar months earlier. John discovered the box in a dark and dusty corner of the railway station. Merrill wouldn't think of laundry until the clean sheets ran out and Muriel was too ill to care.

Inspecting the buildings, we found a leak in the White House roof and the copper guttering for Dollywood had been awaiting installation for six years. The White House, the Manager's House and the two adjacent log cabins had been unused for years and required in-depth cleaning. On this tour of inspection we came across a small building, far removed from any other, with a sign over the door which read, "The Royal York Hotel." Inside was a flush toilet still in working order. I thought it quite remarkable to find a flushie deep in the woods, but it was there to serve the log cabins which had disappeared long ago.

The Goggin cabin, a one-room structure with fireplace and water supply, was to be my accommodation. Several logs at the back had rotted away into the bank. It had to be jacked up and logs were inserted to replace the rotten ones. Next door was the Lewis cabin, named for Ivor Lewis, advertising manager at Eaton's, who had stayed there long years ago when the Inn was in operation. This one-room cabin was where the children and their nanny, John's niece Carol Brown, were to stay. Well, she wasn't really their nanny. She was there to keep an eye on Janet and David, make sure they were safe, amuse them and be sure they didn't drown. She was only thirteen and I promised her $25 at the end of the season, which I was able to pay. Merrill advised that he could provide only $75 as start-up money. I replied that since we had started our business with only $30 cash I couldn't see a problem.

Early in May, leaving John to cope with the business and the care and feeding of the children, I spent a week in the Cement House with Clara Wood of Northbrook and Johnnie Spicer, a carpenter from Flinton. The biggest job Clara and I had was cleaning the ancient Bon Ami off dozens of window panes. We cleaned floors, walls, arranged furniture, hung curtains and sometimes, if he was in a good mood, Mike helped too. Johnnie Spicer repaired the White House roof and helped put the Goggin cabin in livable condition. I bought a used ice box for the Goggin and John replaced the hand basin with a sink and drainboard. Muriel's desk was brought over from her upstairs office in Dollywood because I still had to type Merrill's manuscripts. I was busy and I was pregnant.

Advertising in *The Globe And Mail* led to an enquiry from a man asking for a description of the place because he and his wife spent their honeymoon at Bon Echo in 1927. I told Merrill of this, but he couldn't recall the name until he suddenly remembered that they had changed their name. Originally it was Piddle. They came twice to Bon Echo and stayed in Greystones which, with six bedrooms, was the largest rental cottage. That cost $100 a week just for the two of them. They brought their beautiful Great Dane and their monogrammed highball glasses. The initial was "F."

Every weekend, until Janet's school term was over, John and I were at Bon Echo completing last-minute chores, welcoming the Saturday arrivals and making sure they were comfortable. By the end of June, with most of the cottages booked, Janet, David and Carol took over the Lewis cabin. I moved into the Goggin cabin where, depending upon where you stood, you could be in the office, the bedroom, the living room, the dining room or the kitchen. John was left at home to keep Savigny Electric going and look after himself. He came to Bon Echo only at weekends.

Saturdays were hectic, with families moving out in the mornings, cottages to be cleaned and ready for families coming in in the afternoons. It was imperative that I try to keep Mike in good humour, but his patience was sorely tried when one family demanded four frying pans. They must have planned to catch a lot of fish. Through the week, when he delivered the wood, ice and coal oil to me, he filled me in on the goings-on in the various cottages. Sometimes he made friends with the guests and he'd be invited to dinner or to a wiener roast on the beach. If he was in a good mood he'd bring flowers to me and the more favoured guests. His garden was in an open sunny spot near the barn. In the old days Muriel used to order seeds to be sent to him and the flowers were intended to grace Dollywood and Greystones. Then, only the perennials were left: sweet williams, phlox and peonies.

Sometimes it was one long grumble from Mike, as when someone stored fish on the ice in an ice box. "By Jinjuss, how'm I gonna get the smell out?"

One of Mike's additional responsibilities was the ancient water system, parts of which may have dated from the turn of the century when Dr. Price owned the Inn. Three-inch galvanized pipe, on a pair of wagon wheels rolled way out into the lake, fed water to a pumphouse (not far from the present MNR pump-house) near the Inn site. A large pump driven by a Massey-Harris tractor engine pumped water uphill to a two-thousand-gallon pressure tank. Fifteen or twenty minutes of pumping each evening would normally supply the next day's water. The tractor engine was a perk from Massey-Harris when Merrill was writing *Harvest Triumphant*. On warm summer days the water in the iron pipes laid out around the north beach became hot enough by early evening to wash dishes and for one person to take a bath in Dollywood or Greystones—the only cottages boasting bath tubs.

It was bad news when someone inadvertently left a toilet running and Mike had to tramp around to find out why the water tank was low and then pump more water from the lake. Sometimes, though, the water loss was caused by a leak in the old iron piping which snaked all around the property and beneath the driveway to the White House and the Manager's House. Having assured himself that all the guests were innocent of leaving a tap or toilet running, Mike cut himself a hazel divining rod in a V shape. Holding the stick firmly in both hands, thumbs pointing outward, he began a slow march over the ground. Usually, the leak was in the pipe under the driveway where vehicles had travelled. When the point of the twig pointed downward Mike dug a hole and there, without fail, was the leaking pipe. I was amazed when I first saw this phenomenon. Mike tried his best to teach me how to do it but I just wasn't born with that gift.

In spite of my first impression of Bon Echo, I was falling under its spell. Almost everyone does. As Merrill had written in the Inn's brochure, "It is impossible to describe the magnificence of this scene ... The sand beaches are wonderful, almost as good as the beach at Great Yarmouth, Norfolk, where I played as a child and the tide doesn't come in twice a day to prevent one from enjoying it."

With the kinks ironed out, our routine became established and we all enjoyed the long, hot summer. Janet and David made friends with the visiting children. I had the opportunity to meet many interesting people. The sort of people who enjoy holidays

1954 1954 1954 1954 1954 1954 1954 1954 1954 1954

Ed Davis sanding the skiff, 1954.

in the backwoods, who enjoy lamplight, firelight and cooking on a wood stove, are usually interesting people. The Donald Camfields, then of Ottawa, wrote to say that if the cottages were modernized and electricity was installed they wouldn't be interested in returning.

Of course, the days weren't always sunny. One particularly dreary, rainy afternoon I built a fire to cheer us. As we all knew, a large toad lived in between the hearth stones and, as his premises warmed up, he hopped out to sit out of danger. He seemed quite tame. Carol toasted marshmallows at the fire and I sat squeezed into the child's wooden rocking chair which was really meant for David. Mike came to the door with an unknown lady and gentleman who had come to see the Denisons. As they stood just inside the door I rose to meet them. The little rocking chair came up with me. There we were; children toasting marshmallows, a big fat toad sitting on the hearth, pregnant me with a chair on my backside and, as though on cue, a squirrel ran around the cabin's top log. Not a scene they'd expected at all. Mike chuckled, the two strangers turned and left. I have no idea who they were, but I've often wondered.

Though we had no way of knowing, the future of Bon Echo hung in the balance one Sunday afternoon in August. The cottages were full. Greystones and the Cement House were occupied by friends of the Holloways from New York City. They were writers, journalists and their families and one, named Chaplin, was bemoaning his loss of the editorship of *Collier's Magazine* which had then ceased publication. They were fishing, swimming, drinking and having a good time. Having consumed a sufficient quantity of gin and tomato juice, one of the men climbed on the diving platform which was a hundred feet from shore and there lay face down, sans bathing trunks. No one was much concerned, except John feared he would have a painful sunburn. Into this peaceful scene, down the steps from his cottage, Mike was seen escorting four people, one older couple and one younger. We watched them descending the steps to the beach and saw one of them point to the nude man on the raft. They turned and stumbled back up the steps, nearly knocking Mike off his feet.

The significance of all this we learned more than twenty years later. John and I were making a business call to Beulah and Wilton Foster on Kashawakamak Lake. They had owned their property, Foster's Point, since 1954 and, getting along in years, were ready to sell. To our surprise they told us they had thought of buying Bon Echo when Merrill Denison had it listed for sale for $50,000 in 1954. With younger friends they had gone to inspect the property one Sunday afternoon. When they saw the scene on the beach with little children playing in the sand and adults sitting there obviously unconcerned about the naked man in their midst, they were shocked and left immediately. The Fosters didn't buy Bon Echo, they bought shoreline on Kashawakamak Lake. We had not known that Merrill was so desperate he would have sold his inheritance for $50,000. How different the story would have been if that New York journalist hadn't been lying on the raft.

Although our efforts at Bon Echo didn't make us rich and Savigny Electric actually suffered because of John's frequent absence, we did show a profit. Mike had his wages, Barrie

Township had their taxes, the cottages were in better repair than they had been in years. As well, Merrill and I were a few hundred dollars to the good. Janet, David and Carol had a happy, healthy summer. In fact, forty years later, Carol still tells us that it was one of the best summers she ever had.

By letter of the 24th August, Barry Holloway told us Merrill had that day taken Muriel to a Toronto nursing home. "They flew up with a nurse. It was a hard decision that Merrill had to make but the situation had become intolerable. She is so weak that I am afraid she can't last too long."[10] Barry and Jane planned to come to Bon Echo as soon as possible "as Jane is completely exhausted what with her experience with Muriel the last few weeks."[11]

Jane and Barry arrived at the end of August. Hunter and his girl friend came too, as did Adelaide and Ed Davis from San Marino, California. Adelaide was an old school friend of Jane's and millionaire Ed was chief of Union Carbide. To take command of the kitchen in the Cement House, Clara Wood and her daughter, Laura, were called in. We were able to enjoy some time

Bath time for John Merrill on Dollywood Terrace, 1955.

with the Holloways and their guests as the summer season wound down. Before the Davis' arrival Jane told me Adelaide had a peculiar habit when travelling in that she didn't use suitcases but packed all her clothes in dress boxes. Sure enough, like the little foxes, all her hankies and everything else were in cardboard boxes. And, like the princess and the pea, she loathed the lumpy flock mattress on her bed in Greystones. Forthwith, a box spring and mattress were ordered from Tweed, for which she was pleased to pay. That was the first modern mattress ever enjoyed at Bon Echo.

Ed made himself busy. He put one of the skiffs up on two saw horses, sanded and painted it. They were all able to relax and had good fun. Adelaide was concerned that I should enjoy some relaxation too. Each evening she heated water on the wood stove, filling all the pans she could find, so that I could relax in a warm bath in the Greystones bathtub. With her perfumed soap and talcum powder it was a lovely treat for me.

By mid-September Jane and Barry were the only guests. On the 23rd they were fishing on the Skootamatta River, near Flinton, when Merrill phoned from Toronto to tell us of Muriel's death. John went to find the Holloways and this necessitated borrowing a canoe. He had never paddled a canoe before, but the urgency of the situation almost made him forget his apprehension. Jane and Barry left that day to be with Merrill in Toronto. After the funeral service they all returned to Bon Echo.

The obituary in *The Toronto Daily Star* noted, "Muriel Goggin Denison died on the 23rd September, 1954. She was educated at Havergal College, Edgehill, Windsor, N.S., and studied music at London and Toronto. She was an Anglican and governor of St. Hilda's College, U of T." A service was held in the chapel of the Toronto Crematorium. Muriel and Merrill had been married for twenty-eight years.

A few days later John and I were at Bon Echo to attend the simple ceremony of scattering Muriel's ashes in the Mazinaw. With us were Lizzie and Harry Levere from Cloyne. Over the years they had both been very helpful to the Denisons. Lizzie was a McCausland, a little lady with a big, generous heart, and their two families had a long connection of service at Bon Echo, going back to the time of Merrill's mother. Harry's father had been the caretaker years before.

Mike had two skiffs ready at the water's edge. I followed Merrill across the beach and saw that he was clutching a small cardboard box under his arm. Realizing that the urn must be inside, it occurred to me that someone should offer to open the box and carry it for Merrill, but I didn't want to interfere. He wanted this last duty for himself. Harry rowed the boat carrying Merrill, Jane and Barry. Mike rowed the boat carrying Lizzie, John and me. In front of the huge inscription, dedicated by Merrill's mother to the democratic ideals of Walt Whitman, we stopped. Merrill read a few words from Tennyson's *Crossing The Bar* and from Walt Whitman's *Leaves of Grass*. Then he leaned over the gunwale and tenderly placed the box overboard. It didn't sink. It floated. "Good grief," I thought, "What shall we do now?" Merrill calmly reached out, retrieved the box and tore it open. Then he held it down in the water until it sank.

After returning to New York City with the Holloways, Merrill had some catching up to do. He sent the final Molson chapters and suggested in the accompanying letter that if my baby was a girl he hoped we'd name her Muriel, if a boy, Merrill. John Merrill Savigny was born on the 24th November, 1954. On the 1st of December Merrill and Mister Boo were off visiting old friends and from the home of Donald Moffat in Brookline, Massachusetts, he wrote:

Dear Mary,

Congratulations and hail to John Merrill Savigny. May he live long to enjoy happiness and riches. My own prospects with respect to the latter have been considerably improved since I last saw you. Passing through Montreal last week there was dropped in my lap in a pleasant thirty minute interview the best assignment yet, no less than a commission to undertake the history of the Bank of Montreal. The Holloways have probably already passed the news on to you. All I've ever known about banking and finance has been tinged with the red of over-draughts, or is it drafts, but that cannot deter me; I wasn't much of a brewer or distiller three long years ago. There's nothing much new to report otherwise except that Boo and I have been making pleasant progress. He behaved atrociously at the Drury's, snarling at little children and fighting other dogs. Since then his conduct has been growing more exemplary with each new house he visits and here with the Moffats has been such a paragon of all the canine virtues that they are anxious to adopt him. He has also been elected a member of the exclusive Tavern Club, haunt of Harvard men and bohemians. He's even allowed to play on the English billiard table. Nothing new about Bon Echo nor any change in the plans to carry on next season the same as last. I'll leave here at the end of the week for Stonington and then on to the Holloways where I should reach in about two weeks time. You can reach me there.

The best always,

Merrill"

In January, Merrill came to stay with us and, with our good friends Jane and Don Little, then of Kaladar, became John Merrill Savigny's godparent at St. Paul's Church, Flinton. Though he objected to the church's presumption that our baby had inherited "fault and corruption," he was a thoughtful and generous godfather to our son.

The 1955 season at Bon Echo was to be a busy one and Merrill was able to be there frequently. His office and personal belongings were in Dollywood and if I and the children moved in there I could include Merrill at our family meals, look after the office and free the Goggin for rental. The hitch was that Dollywood had no kitchen. It had two bathrooms, one upstairs and one down, but no kitchen because Dolly Proctor, the lady who had the cottage built during the time the Inn was running, could not abide the smells of cooking. She preferred to walk around to the Inn to take her meals. I don't know who she was, but her name lives on in Dollywood.

In March, Merrill wrote from the Berkeley Hotel, Montreal, "I concur in the idea of making Dollywood headquarters but Barry has a much better idea than yours or any I've had to date. It's one of his amazing qualities, to come out of a gentle alcoholic haze with the simple solution to an involved, knotty problem." Barry's solution was to turn the downstairs bathroom into a kitchen and Earl Hawley, of Northbrook, did just that and, while he was at it, added the screened dining porch overlooking the lake.

My family and I were much more comfortable, of course, than we had been the year before and Merrill didn't seem to mind my cooking. Much to my surprise, he insisted on washing the dishes. He'd whip up masses of Dreft suds, chatter with Janet as she dried the dishes, about the books she was reading and claim it was good therapy. Janet was allowed to borrow any of the books in Merrill's voluminous library and she took full advantage of that opportunity. She confessed recently that, when Dollywood was locked and she couldn't get in the conventional way, she got in through the milk box beside the back door, with a little boost from brother David. She grew up to be a librarian. In the evenings, when the children were in bed, we sat beside the fire with Mister Boo at our feet, while Merrill taught me to play cribbage and often told me stories about his childhood and his mother.

4

Mother of Merrill and Priestess of Walt

L ITTLE BY LITTLE, I put together the story of Merrill's mother, Flora MacDonald Denison. I'd often noticed her photograph on the wall in his office, placed beside a framed quotation taken from Arthur Guiterman's *Spake Theodore Roosevelt*: …"The good die young, so men have sadly sung…Who do not know the happier reason why…Is never that they die while they are young…But that the good are young until they die." There had

Two portraits of Flora MacDonald. On the left with baby Merrill.

been a very special relationship between Flora and her son. She was a most remarkable woman, by no means the average, turn-of-the-century submissive wife and mother. Born on the 20th February, 1867, in Prince Edward County, Eastern Ontario, she was familiar with the area to the north east now known as the Land 0' Lakes. As a young woman she was a teacher at the one-room school in the French Settlement, located on the Bridgewater Road, between Actinolite and Flinton.

Her father, George Merrill, a ne'er-do-well with many other children, became involved with Canadian Senator Billa Flint and others interested in mining in the Flinton area. Squandering his wife's inheritance, George inadvisedly invested $10,000 in a bronze mine. Merrill showed me one of the worthless shares. I wondered how George reacted when he realized he'd been duped and discovered that tin and copper make bronze. There's no such thing as a bronze mine. His family was impoverished.

In the early 1890's Flora left for Toronto where she became a dressmaker and later worked for the Robert Simpson Company as head of the ladies tailoring department. In 1892 she married Howard Denison, a commercial traveller, who didn't spend much time at home. In addition to her career, she had other compelling interests. One of the first vocal feminists, she was a staunch supporter of the women's suffrage movement. She became associated with Emiline Pankhurst, the famous English leader of the International Women's Suffrage Union. She discovered the writings of Walt Whitman, whose ideals of democracy and equality of the sexes matched her own.

Expecting her baby and at odds with the Canadian political climate, Flora refused to bear her child in Canada and, with her sister Effa, departed for Detroit where Merrill was born on the 23rd of June, 1893. The two sisters brought the baby back to Toronto shortly thereafter, doubly sure that he could claim U.S. citizenship because his father also was American born. Merrill presented me with his mother's copy of *Whitman's Poetical Works* in which she had written:

"As long as a flag waves over a person disenfranchised on account of sex, that flag is not big enough for me—so long as a church refuses absolute equality to women with men, so long as it closes its pulpits to the natural teachers and preachers of our race, just so long is that church too small for me. Flora MacD Denison."

Merrill was eight years old in 1901 when his parents first took him to Bon Echo Inn. They travelled by the Canadian Pacific Railway from Toronto to Kaladar, thence by horse and wagon to Snider Depot at the south end of the Mazinaw and then by inboard motor boat, named "The Wanderer," to the dock just south of the narrows. It was Flora's first sight of what was to become the focus of her life. She was enthralled by the Mazinaw, which was sometimes called Lake Massanoga, and the magnificent Bon Echo Rock. It was so named because sounds do echo back from it in a most satisfying way. In 1904 Flora was able to buy property on the shore of the lower lake from Catherine Meeks, in Lot 27 in the Second Range of Barrie Township. Descendents of that first Meeks family are still in the Cloyne area, including another Catherine.

Merrill looked back with fondness to his summer holidays on the Mazinaw and his school days in Toronto. Under his mother's careful guidance he grew up in an easy-going, loving atmosphere. Though Flora gave him every opportunity to make his own decisions, he came to accept her philosophy as his own, which did not include adherence to any church or religion. One of Merrill's oft-told stories, when the subject of religion came up, was about the day he decided to go to Sunday School. The real reason was that he could be with his little sweetheart, Violet. The church basement where the children gathered was gloomy and forbidding, the teacher looked stern and unfriendly. Her message about God making heaven and earth and all things in it, including little boys and girls, concluded with the alarming news that God would send you to hell if you didn't measure up. The lad was stunned to hear that the God who made you the way you are, punished you for *being* the way you are. He said he wasted no time in dashing home, leaving Violet and the church forever. His understanding mother told him he could make up his own mind when he was older.

Happier memories were of summers at the Mazinaw cottage and Mary Bey, his baby-sitter, he called her. She was a Mohawk and taught Merrill about her people, about the land and the wild creatures living thereabouts. She built a junior-size birch bark canoe for him which he then still cherished. Her explanation of the Great Spirit known to her people seemed to make more sense than Violet's Sunday School teacher.

In the summer of 1910, back again on the Mazinaw, the Denisons heard that Bon Echo Inn was for sale. Built at the turn of the century by Dr. Weston A. V. Price, a Canadian-born dentist from Cleveland, the Inn was a going concern. The dentist and his wife, Florence, had no thought of selling until their young son, Donald, died suddenly. Flora, then and there, agreed to buy. On the 27th September, 1910, Flora received title to Bon Echo; fourteen parcels of land, for thirteen thousand dollars. Her husband, Howard, is named with her as Grantee in the typewritten document, but his name is stroked out and references to the Grantees as "parties" are altered to read "party." The Toronto solicitor who drew the deed assumed that Howard was to be co-owner. How wrong he was!

Though Howard didn't seem to have much say in the matter, he did help manage the Inn for a couple of summers before Flora found reason to divorce him. She had also found reason to divorce herself from the Robert Simpson Company when they required their employees to punch a time clock. That she considered degrading. She went back to her own dressmaking business and, further promoting her interest in women's rights, she wrote a weekly column for *The Toronto Sunday World*.

In acquiring the Inn, hundreds of acres of land and miles of Lake Mazinaw shoreline, including the Big Rock, Flora was prepared to realize her dream of establishing a summer-time community devoted to the teachings of her idol, Walt Whitman. She had travelled to Camden, New Jersey, to meet Horace Traubel, Whitman's friend and biographer, and found strength and support in him. She encouraged other believers to come to Bon Echo and there she became the founder of The Whitman Club of Bon Echo.

It is from several editions of *The Sunset Of Bon Echo* that I have learned more about Flora. These booklets date from 1916 to 1920. This tireless woman was publisher, editor-in-chief, reporter, copy writer and sales manager. Ostensibly to promote membership in

The Whitman Club, they also blatantly advertise the Inn. Inside the front cover she wrote:

"BON ECHO-SUMMER RESORT. Most picturesque spot in Canada.
Under first-class management.
Fresh milk, butter, eggs and vegetables supplied from the Bon Echo Farm.
Small-mouthed black bass, white fish, and lake salmon are plentiful in Lake Massanoga.
Huckleberries and other wild berries grow in great abundance.
Rates—from 14 to 20 dollars a week. Children half rates.
Special rates for large parties and long stays.
A passport is not needed by Americans entering Canada."

In the first edition of her Whitman Club magazine, Flora tells of her belief in the spirit world and how her booklet came to be named *The Sunset Of Bon Echo*:

"I will write short stories about the people who are living here and now—people who are more or less before the public as leaders or otherwise. I shall try to expose cant and hypocrisy, to the end that through me some wrongs may be righted.

I have been aided so far in my work by friends in the Spirit World and I want to tell you about some of them without explanation or apology.

Mary Merrill was a sister in earth life of Mrs. Denison. She is a great comrade of mine, and has helped me over many stony places.

A Hindu prince is often in communion with me, and his chief concern is the terrible wrongs brought about by unjust caste systems.

Sunset (for whom this little magazine is named) was an Indian Chief. He first became my friend when Mrs. Denison—then Flora Merrill—taught school in the backwoods. He is a healer and has often assisted me in stopping pain through both mental and magnetic healing. 'Crusts-and-Crumbs' has often been my teacher and much has come to me through the spirit of those two columns.[12]

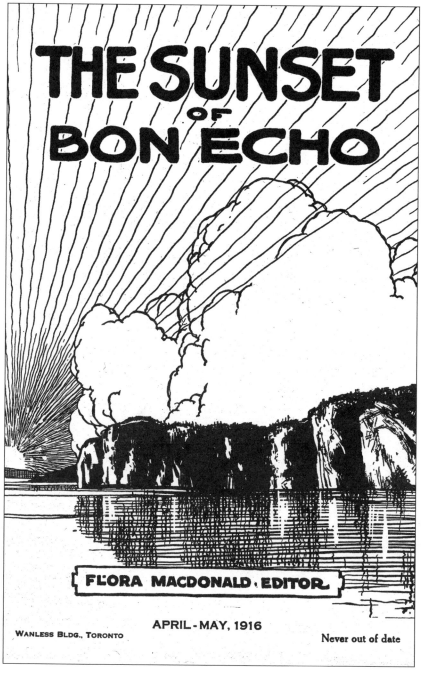

Front cover of Flora's magazine, *The Sunset of Bon Echo*. Designed by Merrill, Signed "Wid", her nickname for him.

THE SUNSET
OF
BON ECHO

· FLORA · MACDONALD ·
EDITOR.

MARCH, 1916

Vol. 1   No. 1

" *The institution of the dear love of comrades.*"
—WALT WHITMAN

The Whitman Club of Bon Echo
Founded by FLORA MACDONALD

" *Neither master nor servant am I.*"—WALT WHITMAN.

THE SUNSET OF BON ECHO is the official organ of the
Whitman Club, edited by Flora MacDonald.
Now the idea, and the why; who was Whitman; what and
where is Bon Echo, and who is Flora Macdonald?

Whitman

CARLYLE, Tennyson, Emerson, Burroughs, Ingersoll, Dr.
Buck, Hubbard and a whole galaxy of lesser lights took off
their mental caps to Walt. Whitman, and with one accord placed
him on a higher pedestal than had been. Whitman is the poet
of that divine democracy which gives equal rights to all the sons
and daughters of this earth.

Life, love, nature, death, all mean more and are more since
Whitman wrote of them.

Men and women mean more and are more since Whitman
founded the institution of the dear love of comrades.

His philosophy and his religion are broader and better than
other ... included all and rejected none.

... t its victory, death lost its sting and life became
... lm of Life in that wondrous book called Leaves

... of Humanity was sung.

Left, The Whitman Club
of Bon Echo Masthead,
Vol. 1, No. 1, March, 1916
Below, Emma Hawley and
Olive Delmage Hawley in
the ladies parlour, Bon
Echo Inn. Small boy
thought to be Donald
Price, son of Dr. and Mrs.
Weston Price
Right above, Bon Echo
Inn. Small boy thought to
be Donald Price.
Right below, view of Upper
Mazinaw from the Bon
Echo Inn verandah.

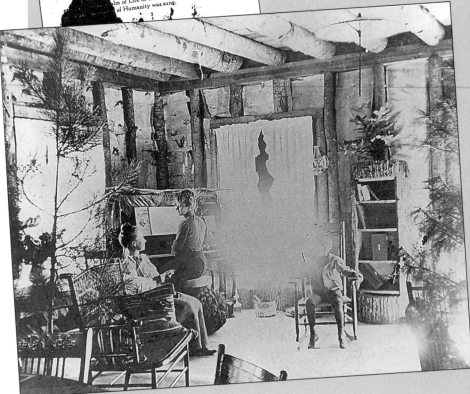

An Arab is a spirit to whom I owe much. His swiftness of decision has helped when problems most perplexed me. Walt Whitman makes the mystic seven complete. These will constitute the personnel of the Sunset. Walt Whitman is the master guide. He has taken me to unbelievable heights and I have neither fear nor anxiety about the future."

Flora mentions "the mystic seven," though I can count only six. Perhaps she herself was the seventh. In the early years of this century the works of Walt Whitman were more widely known and discussed than they are today. Even I knew "O Captain, My Captain" by heart. Whitman's hope for humanity was that "distinctions of caste, colour, race, creed and sex should fade away in the glorious comradeship of brotherhood." Many understood him and were drawn to him but others were repelled. Albert E.S. Smythe who, in 1916, was the first president of The Walt Whitman Fellowship of Toronto, wrote in *The Sunset*;

"Whitman has been accused of grossness and even obscenity, on account of the presence of some dozen lines of a physiological nature in a volume of 450 pages. It is a distorted mentality that refuses to read the Bible because there are dozens of obscene passages in it. It is the intention that soils, and neither in the Bible, nor in *Leaves Of Grass* is this taint of intentional obscenity to be found. That is left to the reader."

By 1916 Merrill's training and interest were leading him to a career as an architect. With the Great War raging in Europe however, he told his mother, as she quoted in *The Sunset*: " ... I feel I must soon get away to France. Whitman thought it worth while to help save life and gave his health and strength to the wounded in the Civil War. I too can do the same, and as an American I can put in my protest individually against the Belgium outrages and the *Lusitania* tragedy, and show that I appreciate what Lafayette did for American Liberty. England then learned a big lesson and Canada's loyalty is due to the fact that while She is a Daughter in her Mother's house, She is Mistress in her own. 'I felt an awful wrench through my soul when he spoke of France, but became quiet as he talked. I so wanted him to go on with his splendid constructive profession, as he knew.'

The prospect of helping in this big game that is being played in

Europe means more than anything that has ever come into my life. Architecture, with this war going on, seems like planting pine cones in the path of a forest fire."

In the 1917 edition of *The Sunset* Flora published a very long letter from Merrill. Her nickname for her son was "Wid" and he called her "Dear Little Min," but I cannot explain the significance of those names. He had not joined a fighting regiment but, like Whitman, chose to serve with the American Ambulance Corps. From "Somewhere in France," he tells of transporting the dead and wounded to the *Poste de Secours*. He happily discovers that one of his crew also belongs to what he calls "the sacred Order of Mother and Son." His new friend, Donald Moffat, brought him a lump of clay which Merrill was delighted to receive and with which he sculpted the head of another of his crew. Moffat remained his friend until his death in the sixties. He was one of several who loaned money to Merrill in the difficult days of the depression.

Merrill never told us much about his service in France except he once remarked that he carried a bucket of iodine and a sponge, the best he could do for the wounded he transported to the field hospital. Digging in the office closet one day, he came across the certificate of appreciation he received from the French Government. This 28"x 25" certificate was still rolled in its mailing tube, addressed to 4 Hayter Street, the Denisons' Toronto home. "Would you like to have it?" he asked John. He didn't seem to take pride in its possession, but we have treasured it over the years.

In 1917 Merrill returned to Canada. Convinced he should now serve with his fellow Americans, he volunteered at Fort Leavenworth and was accepted as a 2nd Lieutenant in an infantry regiment. Again in France, it seems he was mainly occupied escorting German prisoners-of-war by rail from one sector to another. He saw no action. One hilarious story he used to tell involves POWs' escaping from his train and others sneaking aboard believing they would be better off going wherever his train was going. Merrill asked "Der Herr Feldwebel" to count his men at each stop along the way. Starting with, let's say, a hundred and sixty men, he lost two, gained three, lost a few more but arrived in Paris with a hundred and sixty, albeit not all the same men who had started the journey with him. That doesn't sound like a very funny story ,but Merrill's dead-pan delivery and frequent references to "Der Herr Feldwebel" always had his audience in stitches.

Demobilized in Paris at the end of the war, Merrill decided to stay and, under the auspices of the U.S. Government, began architectural studies at the Ecole des Beaux Arts. By 1919 he was in both New York and Boston with architectural firms. One assignment, he liked to relate, was designing an hotel. All went well and he was pleased with his work until he realized the hotel would have to employ waiters no more than four feet tall. Something was wrong with the dimensions of the passageway leading from the kitchen to the dining room.

Throughout the years of the Great War, under Flora's management, the Inn prospered as more and more Whitmanites found their way to Bon Echo. The author of *Cosmic Consciousness*[13], Dr. Richard Maurice Bucke, became her friend. Still on library shelves and still read by students of psychology, his book proposes that Walt Whitman belongs with that illustrious group of few men and fewer women who were aware of their cosmic consciousness. Bucke names Moses, Socrates, Jesus, Paul, Mohammed, Blake and Balzac among others who attained:

"Consciousness of the cosmos, of the life and order of the universe. Intellectual enlightenment or illumination which alone would place the individual on a new plane of existence. State of moral exultation, an indescribable feeling of elevation, elation and joyousness and a quickening of the moral sense. With these come what may be called a sense of immortality, a consciousness of eternal life, not a conviction that he shall have this, but the consciousness that he has it already."

Dr. Bucke, in 1876, was Superintendent of the Provincial Asylum for the Insane in Hamilton, Ontario. In 1882 he was Professor of Mental and Nervous Diseases at Western University in London, Ontario. His humane and revolutionary treatment of the mentally ill brought him recognition in Canada, the U.S. and Europe and a close friendship with Helen Keller.

The magnificent beauty, grandeur, strength and permanence of the Rock made it the symbol of Flora's love for the Good Gray Poet. She determined that it should become a lasting memorial and by 1919 she planned to dedicate the Rock to Walt Whitman. Although he had spent time in Canada with Richard Bucke and others in Ontario, Whitman never saw Bon Echo, but Flora felt his presence there. Whitman's devoted friend, disciple and distinguished biographer was Horace Traubel and Flora invited him to be with her at the ceremony of dedication. Though an ill old man, he and his wife, Anne Montgomerie, made the long, tedious journey from New York to Bon Echo early in August, 1919. His joy is best expressed in the letter he wrote to Flora:

"Letter from Horace Traubel, North Verandah, Bon Echo. Delivered by Mildred Bain to Mrs. Denison at the Kitchen Sink. August 12th, 1919.

Dear Mother of Merrill, dear priestess of Walt, dear comrade of the rest of us:- I take it for granted that you realize, though we haven't given vocal expression to it, that Anne and I appreciate to the full the considerate and generous hospitality you have shown us since we came in, in a thousand ways mental and physical.

Bon Echo seems to have wonders of the seen and the invisible to make a visit with it and you sacredly memorable.

In these days of physical disability, when everybody's doing kindnesses for me and I'm doing nothing for anybody, I acknowledge with pain my consciousness of being a burden and charge to you and Anne and the others. I shrink with humility into the shadow of this confession. In spite of appearances, I still have some hope that I may live to repay in some part the great debt I am so aware I owe to you all.

All things here suggest beauty and seem couched in the broadest human spirit. I can respond to this mentally even if I am unable to do so in deeds of good fellowship. My heart calls me to do that which I am unable to do. In the midst of so much that is mystic and mighty and humanly inclusive I stand helpless and pitiful.

I trust dear Flora that though I haven't had the courage to even try to put this into sentences of daily speech I am still overflowing in the unspoken response of affection and gratitude.

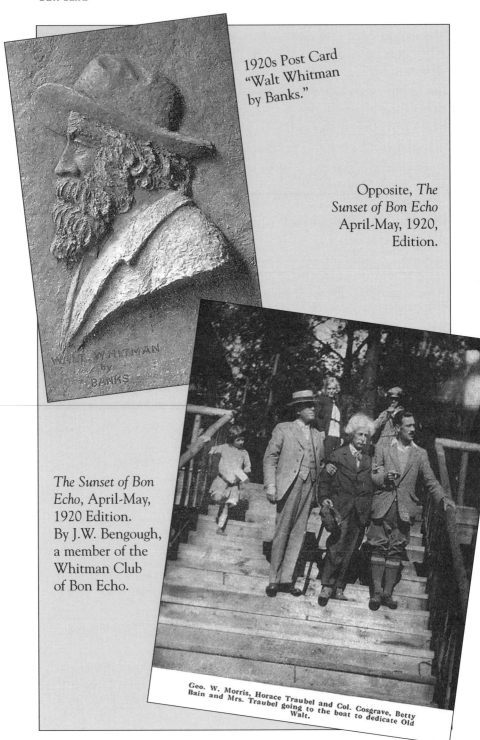

1920s Post Card
"Walt Whitman
by Banks."

Opposite, *The
Sunset of Bon Echo*
April-May, 1920,
Edition.

*The Sunset of Bon
Echo,* April-May,
1920 Edition.
By J.W. Bengough,
a member of the
Whitman Club
of Bon Echo.

Geo. W. Morris, Horace Traubel and Col. Cosgrave, Betty
Bain and Mrs. Traubel going to the boat to dedicate Old
Walt.

A Welcome to Horace Traubel
By J. W. Bengough

Dear comrade Horace, Bon Echo welcomes you;
The old frame Inn, of honest, democratic pine-boards,
Knowing nothing of the floor-polish, shining mahogany counters,
    modern improvements of the fashionable hotel.
But eloquent of the soul of things; of the good old days of home-
    spun,
Emphasizing the facts, and yet with the unmatchable poetry of
    rustic construction of tree-trunk pillars and birch-bark
    wainscoting—
The old pine-board Inn welcomes you, and throws the arms of
    friendship and hospitality around you;
And this green, breezy peninsula in which she stands amid   her
    grove of maples and pines and oaks,
(More to the heart of her than any classic grove of Greece could
    ever be)
Bids you welcome;
You, whose name is known and honored;

2

I only want your institution to understand my unspoken love. The best thought of the soul is never uttered, the best sentiments of the heart are never put into words.

Mendelssohn wrote songs without words as he called them. Let my sensations of this moment be taken by you as fraternal feelings without words.

Let it stand as that final substance of truth which shame the efforts of the best words to compass.

Always with joy,

Horace Traubel"

On the 25th of August, Horace seemed well enough to join with Flora and perhaps fifteen other members of the Whitman Club in their dedication of the Rock. Flora's emotional account in *The Sunset* tells of the frail old man being helped into one of the boats and being rowed with her through the narrows to the face of the Rock. The others followed in various rowboats and

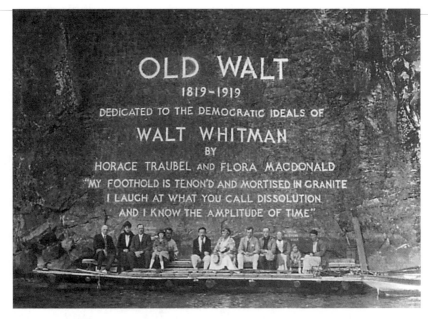

Flora under the "P". Merrill with small girl on his lap, 1919.

canoes. Placing their hands on the Rock, Flora and Horace pronounced the words, "Old Walt."

Weakened and ill after the dedication ceremony, Horace was put to bed and tenderly cared for by Anne, Flora, Merrill and the others. Flora tells us that Horace clearly saw Walt's head and shoulders over the Rock and heard him calling, "Come on." She saw a huge eagle circling round and round and thought of Ingersoll calling Whitman an eagle soaring above the theological chickadees and sparrows. At five o' clock in the afternoon of the 5th of September, Horace joined Walt Whitman.

Merrill told us what happened next. He drove a team and democrat wagon to Hawley Stone's store in Flinton to buy a coffin. There was some difficulty because Hawley wasn't there and his daughter was reluctant to part with what must have been a substantial item of inventory. Presumably, Merrill didn't have the necessary cash. Speed was essential because they were intending to get Horace, with Anne and Flora, on the midnight train, but it was slow going, through pouring rain, over the rough road back to Bon Echo. Nevertheless, they arrived at Kaladar in time to stop the train. That was done, and was still done for years thereafter, by swinging a lamp provided for the purpose, back and forth beside the track when the train was heard approaching. With Horace stowed in the baggage car, Merrill saw the sad women off to New York, via Montreal. He followed them later.

A New York community church was chosen for Horace's funeral service several days later and Flora was arranging the many wreaths of flowers when she heard someone yell, "Fire!" The organ loft was ablaze. Horace's cortege had not yet arrived. Flora heard a voice from the crowd in the street, "He'd burn the church down rather than be found inside." After hurried consultation, the cortege was re-directed across town to a school auditorium where the service was finally conducted. Horace's body was later laid to rest near his home in Camden, New Jersey.

Returning to Bon Echo, Flora and Merrill were in time to oversee the two Scottish stone masons who had been brought over from Aberdeen to chisel Old Walt's memorial on the face of the Rock. Flora had chosen the words many years before from "Song of Myself," one of the poems in *Leaves Of Grass*. Horace Traubel, at the earlier dedication ceremony, had told Flora, "That was an inspiration. Walt must have had a prophetic vision when he wrote those lines. Of all Whitman you have picked just the right words." The stone masons carved the inscription:

OLD WALT
1819 - 1919
DEDICATED TO THE DEMOCRATIC IDEALS OF
WALT WHITMAN
BY
HORACE TRAUBEL AND FLORA MACDONALD
"MY FOOTHOLD IS TENON'D AND MORTISED IN
GRANITE
I LAUGH AT WHAT YOU CALL DISSOLUTION
AND I KNOW THE AMPLITUDE OF TIME"

One hundred years after Walt Whitman's birth, Flora was able to rejoice and know that generations later those words would still be read and understood by all who value democracy.

Merrill returned to his architectural endeavours and Flora stayed on at Bon Echo. She wrote the following for publication in her Whitman magazine, The Sunset Of Bon Echo:

"The Night The North Lake Froze Over
Alone in the Cement Cottage, December 13th, 1919
By Flora MacDonald

At 1.30 p.m. Mary and I had gone out to the Perry Road, where I posted over three hundred greetings to folks I knew and for reasons whom I wanted to remember me.

The cold was then beginning to close in. It was after three when we got back and I prepared a good meal for myself, Mac and Jim (my dog and cat). I then brought in the wood for the night, huge lumps of maple I could just lift; smaller sticks of birch and poplar and lots of resinous smelling pine for kindling. The three mile walk in the clear crisp air had put such life and vim in me that the wood carrying was too easy and I split up many a huge lump, intended for the fire-place, and made stove wood of it, and I sawed several cedar poles, all just for the joy of being strong enough to do it.

I carried water, I made cookies, ten dozen, just because I had received a recipe from Maggie and I wanted to see how they would turn out. They are fine and I'll have the fun of giving most of them away. It was 10 p.m. before I thought of eats again and I wondered what I'd have. I finally decided on a sandwich. I remembered the wonderful Copenhagen sand-wiches and I began by boiling an egg hard. Then I took a small onion, then a bit of cold ham, a little mustard, pepper and salt and chopped it all very fine. I buttered two slices of thin bread, placed the gorgeous stuffing between them and sprinkled the whole with a little paprika. I never tasted any-thing so good in all my life. There is just one room downstairs in the cottage 20 x 22, but I boiled the egg in the kitchen, ate in the dining room and drank a demitasse of coffee by the old rose-wood table in front of the fireplace.

I picked up one bit of reading after another, finally re-reading the May "Conservator." Then I read out loud much of Whitman's "Song of Myself," "So Long" and "To My Soul." Eleven - twelve - one o' clock. Every half hour or so I'd go out, the cold was tightening. At 10.30 the moon rose in the north-east directly over "Old Walt," the lake was calm and the shadow of the Great Rock, with snow clinging to all its rough places, was perfect in its reflections. At one o'clock it was 20 below zero and the lake was almost frozen over. I stood at its edge and watched it for a long time, creeping, creeping inch by inch till at 1.30 it had reached the western shore. The lower lake was frozen over a week ago, but I always loved the north lake best because "Old Walt" reflected here its grandeur and solidity, its majesty and mys-tery - its millions of years of becoming, and how it did rebel against the Frost king and his strength to bind it fast. It snapped and crackled.

It is two o'clock - great logs are on the fire and the stove is red hot. The dog (a wonderful Boston) and cat are cosy in down cushions.

I read again Neitzsche's idea of a superman. On such a night as this a superman should get ideas that would make him a veritable god. I'll go to bed and sleep with my window open, the moon and the stars fairly snapping with brilliancy shining in, the whiteness of the snow making very high lights, the blackness of the pines making very deep shadows.

This day and this night has squared the account of many meaningless days.
I say the body is not more than the soul
And the soul is not more than the body
And nothing, not God
Is greater to one than oneself is.
Walt Whitman "

Flora and her son were together at Bon Echo for only one more season. Merrill left the States disenchanted with his prospects as an architect. At the University of Toronto his friend, Roy Mitchell, who was the first director of Hart House Theatre, urged him to take on the position of art director and set designer for the theatre. There, quite by chance, his future course was set. He discovered that he could write. It's now a well-known story that in the spring of 1921 Merrill and several of his colleagues, including Roy Mitchell, planned to produce three Canadian plays but they had only two. Merrill announced that the only true Canadians were the sort he knew in the Ontario backwoods and he saw no problem in writing a play about them. His fiendish friends locked him in an office, told him the dining room closed at two o'clock and challenged him to write the required play. *Brothers-In-Arms* was that play and Merrill was released in time for lunch.

Just when Flora's star was shining brightest, when she had realized her dream of dedicating the Rock to Old Walt for all to see, when she had her most beloved son back again from the horrors of war, she caught a cold in the chilly first days of the season at Bon Echo. Pneumonia developed and Merrill took her back to Toronto. Flora was only fifty-four years old, but must have known she was dying. She probably had not made a will because on the 19th of May she signed a deed conveying to Merrill all her properties in the

Township of Barrie in the County of Frontenac. Her shaky signature shows how ill she must have been and is witnessed by Marguerite Manley, Graduate Nurse. Flora died on the 23rd of May, 1921.

Merrill mourned the loss of his precious mother, dear comrade and best friend. Inheriting Bon Echo, he accepted what he considered to be his sacred trust. That was to hold the property intact, to ensure that it be enjoyed in perpetuity by all and any who wished to be there: all people of any race, colour or creed; employer, employee; rich or poor.

5

The Dream of Bon Echo: A Place of Meeting

ALTHOUGH we did have those quiet summer evenings in Dollywood when Merrill reminisced about the old days, the 1955 season was a busy one for me. Reservations were coming in, many from families who had enjoyed being at Bon Echo the previous year. The housekeeping resort idea of Barry Holloway's was working.

In anticipation of a capacity crowd I had ordered seven hundred blocks of ice. On an appointed day in February, Russell Brown of Twin Pines Resort on Mississagagon Lake, arrived with his ice-cutting crew and equipment. His WW2 army truck and snow plough were used to plough his way in from Highway 41, clear off a suitable area of the lake and plough the road to the icehouse. The ice that year was an ideal twenty inches thick. An old rotary saw with an engine mounted on wheels was set to cut almost through the ice. When sufficient rows of identical blocks were cut, each about a hundred pounds, they were broken off with pike poles and floated to an elevator belt which raised them to the truck. Alternate layers of sawdust and ice were packed on what remained of last year's ice and by late afternoon the whole pile of about 70,000 pounds was carefully covered and the crew departed to perform the same routine at lake after lake until their contracts were completed. The cost of that day's operation was $97 and $10 for the sawdust from Sawyer-Stoll's mill.

Again with Clara Wood's help, the cottages had been made ready for guests. Clean curtains were hung at the windows; rugs, blankets and linens were unpacked from the tin closets. Dollywood, with its new kitchen, was now fully functional and I soon realized we had made the alterations not a day too soon.

Dollywood and Mike.

Early in the year Merrill had been investigating the scope of research required for his history of the Bank of Montreal. He had access to their records at the head office in Montreal and to archives in Ottawa. He realized it was a formidable challenge and almost gave up. He said he had been asked, "How much is this going to cost?" and had replied, "It's like buying a yacht. If you have to ask, you can't afford it." No one knew it was going to be twelve years later that the final chapter would be written. *The Barley And The Stream* was completed, but *The Power To Go* was still in the works. Christy Borth, Merrill's contact with the American Auto-mobile Manufacturers' Association in Detroit, had distributed the manuscript among a group of school children and asked them to underline all the words they couldn't understand. The result was a frustrating re-write. Merrill invariably had at least two books and other time-consuming commitments to juggle at any one time, but as long as there was a supply of paper on hand, a typewriter or a pencil, he continued his self-discipline of writing almost every day.

One of Merrill's other commitments was to pursue his dedication to the trust he had accepted upon his mother's death. Now
almost sixty-two, he felt an urgency to fulfill the dream of Bon
Echo becoming a self-sustaining meeting place, a conference centre. Lake Mazinaw was variously called Massanoga and Mishinog
by the aboriginal and early European settlers. However pronounced, the name means Place of Meeting. According to Merrill
it had been a meeting place for the Iroquois and Algonquins and
on occasion unfriendly meetings occurred, as times when warriors
fought to the death atop the Rock. He said, tongue in cheek, that
Indian maidens in birch bark canoes kept score of bodies flung
into the lake. One can still see the counting marks they made on
the Rock with their fingers dipped in red ochre! Indeed, the pic-
tographs along the face of the Rock, at canoe height, are still
unexplained, so Merrill may have been right.

By mid-April it became clear to me that important negotiations were going on and that Merrill was close to his goal. Bon
Echo was to become again the Place of Meeting. Representatives
of Canadian labour unions, agricultural and forestry associations,
cultural and education groups were in conference and the decision had been made that they would all meet together at Bon
Echo on the 16th of May. John Labatt was invited too. His brewery had agreed to foot the bill for the initial study.

Meanwhile, in Montreal, Merrill had taken time out to be with
old friends and soon made new ones, particularly at the Montreal
Press Club. Not very long after he was settled in Montreal,
Merrill met Nancy Palmer. She was thirty-seven years old, an
American divorcee with two young daughters away in boarding
school. A tall, attractive, self-possessed brunette, she had gone to
Montreal believing a job awaited her there. There was no job but
she found Merrill; an amusing and sympathetic companion. She
thought he was wealthy and Merrill didn't advise her otherwise.
He enjoyed her and she was able to bring him out of his mourn-
ing for Muriel. A new day had dawned.

Jack F. Peterson, an employee of John Labatt Limited, was
Executive Director of the newly-formed Bon Echo Foundation.
His task was to bring together this disparate group of people who
were expected to finance and direct the creation of a centre for

the educational and cultural use of their various unions and asso-
ciations. It was a monumental task. At the 16th of May meeting
Merrill would announce the gift of his vast land holdings to the
Bon Echo Foundation, in trust, for the people of Ontario.

Jack came to see us in April to explain his position and ask for our
help. He expected over thirty visitors plus press people, local township and county representatives to attend. The problem he had for
us to solve was feeding them. We thought of our friend, Ted
Courneya, until recently the owner of the Northbrook Hotel, then
owner of the Tweedsmuir Hotel in Tweed. He and his wife, Dora,
would know how to prepare a good meal with only the Cement
House wood stove for cooking, but they were thirty-five miles away.
Nevertheless, they rose to the occasion. Ted decided to serve roast
beef, baked ham, salads and sand-baked beans, with pies for dessert.

No one had ever heard of sand-baked beans, but we trusted
Ted. The day before the gathering, he asked Mike to dig a hole in
the sand on the shore in front of the Cement House and have the
kindling and wood ready for the fire. John was the selfless one
who volunteered to get the fire going at five o'clock in the morning. Ted arrived about eight o'clock with the beans in two huge
lidded iron pots. They were lowered into the hole, covered with
hot embers and the sand was replaced.

Jack Peterson had asked John to have finger boards printed
with BON ECHO in large type and they were nailed to trees
pointing the way up Highway 41 from Kaladar. The guests were
arriving from Ottawa, Montreal, Toronto and London and Jack
didn't want them to lose their way. The representative from the
Department of Lands and Forests knew his way. He came by
plane. Merrill, in great good humour, wore his MacDonald kilt, a
recent item in his wardrobe. He and Nancy greeted the guests.
The young and handsome John Labatt came in with a more-than-
ample supply of his company's product which most of the guests
lost no time in sampling.

The unique aspect of this meeting was that never before had
the leaders of the Canadian Congress of Labour and the Trades
and Labour Congress agreed to speak to each other, let alone
break bread together. The CCL was represented by A.R. (Pappy)
Mosher, the TLC by the urbane Claude Jodoin. Other important

John Labatt, Merrill Denison, Claude Jodoin, A.R. Mosher, Dr. H.H. Hannam, May 1955.

attendees included Bert Hepworth of the Canadian Brotherhood of Railway Employees, Dr. H.H. Hannam of the Canadian Federation of Agriculture, Gordon Cushing of the TLC, John Kidd of the Canadian Citizenship Council, Merrill's old friend, James A. Cowan of the Canadian Film Institute, Reeve Jack Head of Barrie Township and Edward Morley, Warden of Lennox & Addington County. Sam Curry, owner and editor of *The Tweed News* was there. *The Associated Press* photographer, Nat Turofsky, then well-known in the newspaper business, came too. Realizing that some were taking advantage of the free beer and may not look their best for much longer, Turofsky very sensibly guided his subjects down to the beach and then into Dollywood and arranged them in friendly-looking groups to be photographed.

All were curious about the sand-baked beans and gathered around to watch the iron pots being lifted from the hole in the beach. Lunch in the Cement House was an unqualified success,

Greystones looking north, 1955.

The Cement House, 1955.

served by Ted Courneya and his good-natured helpers. The speeches afterwards were brief and Merrill verbally gave Bon Echo to the people of Canada.

There was no formal meeting of the group, they just wandered about and, going into Dollywood, I found Pappy Mosher holding forth in the kitchen. He grabbed all of my ninety-eight pounds and plunked me on his chubby knee. Not wishing to offend, I decided to grin and bear it. At that moment Merrill came in. His look of astonished disapproval was withering. As soon as I could disentangle myself from Pappy's embrace, I went to find Merrill who had left in disgust. I explained, "You said you wanted us all to be kind and polite to these people, and I was."

In a day or two John heard from Jack Peterson:

"Thank you for the magnificent help you and Mary gave me on Monday. I know you went to a lot of trouble and it is appreciated.

Well, the project is off to a good start and now it's up to me to keep it rolling. The Press coverage we got was truly astounding. We hit the front page of *The Globe and Mail*, *The Ottawa Citizen*, and had really good stories in all the dailies. Even this soon the reaction has been quite astounding.

Mother and I had a most delightful trip back to Toronto— an hour and ten minutes from Bon Echo—and then Turofsky and I worked until four o'clock Tuesday morning getting out pictures and cutlines. We got *Canadian Press* to accept two pictures in Canada, sent out other pictures to all the agricultural and labour papers.

Everyone here and in London thinks Ted Courneya did a wonderful job on the meal. So do I—it was even better than I anticipated.

I'm going away to the States this coming week to study similar projects—don't know how long I'll be gone. Then it will be a matter of speaking to all kinds of groups, drumming up interest across the country, and planning what we are going to build.

P.S. Did Merrill succeed in prying the bottle of whiskey out of Mike? I hope not."

In order to assess the possible development of the Bon Echo property, Jack visited five U.S. centres, each offering differing facilities for a wide range of interest. The largest camp was Chautauqua, near Buffalo in New York State, which began operating as a church camp in 1873. A camp for the United Automobile Workers was Camp Roosevelt on Lake Huron. The International Ladies' Garment Workers had a recreation centre at Unity House in the Pocono Mountains, Pennsylvania. Camp Tamement, close to Unity House, offered the general public recreation and musical entertainment. Tanglewood in the Berkshires was a popular music centre operated by the Boston Symphony Orchestra.

Jack's subsequent report made recommendations for the development of Bon Echo, including models worth copying and pitfalls to avoid. The lengthy report was sent to members of the Bon Echo Foundation:

Barry J. Holloway, Vice President, The Grolier Society Inc., New York, New York

Dr. Algernon D. Black, New York Ethical Culture Society, New York, New York

Merrill Denison, Montreal

John Kidd, Canadian Citizenship Council, Ottawa

Hugh A. Mackenzie, John Labatt Limited, London, Ontario

David Kirk, Canadian Federation of Agriculture, Ottawa

James A. Cowan, Canadian Film Institute, Toronto

J. A.C. Cropley, Deep River Community Association, Deep River

Dr. J. Roby Kidd, Canadian Association for Adult Education, Toronto

Gordon Cushing, Trades & Labour Congress of Canada, Ottawa

Walter L. Gordon, President, Woods and Gordon Limited, Toronto

J.F. Peterson, Executive Director, Bon Echo Committee, Toronto

W.B. Greenwood, Chief, Division of Parks, Department of Lands & Forests, Queen's Park, Toronto

The last man on the list eventually became the most influential of the group. Though Labatts were by then financing what might be termed the feasibility study, this did not interfere with my continuing to rent the cottages. Before the first guests arrived, however, another large gathering was planned. The Canadian Authors' Association (CAA) was to have a conference in Kingston. Merrill said their members planned a bus trip to Bon Echo on the 29th of June, to celebrate the one-hundredth anniversary of the publication of Walt Whitman's *Leaves Of Grass*. He advised that three of Nancy's friends would soon arrive at Bon Echo to help Mike around the place and generally make themselves useful.

The children and I had not yet moved to Bon Echo for the season so I was not much involved with the three men. They were John J. Hunt, Norman Namerow and Richard Pascal who, it was said, was the son of a well-known Montreal hardware merchant. Their most lasting accomplishment that week, presumably with Merrill's permission, was to rig ropes on the ringbolts above the inscription and paint the chiselled letters with aluminum paint. When I saw what they'd done, I was dismayed. Old Walt looked like a billboard, but I had to admit it was readable from the beach across the bay.

There were several coincidences which had been noted by Barry Holloway, who was then Public Relations Vice President of the Grolier Society and also a member of the Bon Echo Foundation. The Canadian Authors' Association convention in Kingston, so conveniently timed, provided an ideal opportunity to further the aims of the foundation. The Grolier Society Inc., publishers of *The Book Of Knowledge* and based in New York City, had recently opened a Canadian publishing house in Toronto and were anxious to advertise their *Encyclopedia Canadiana*. Barry's master stroke was to tie it all to the first publication of Walt Whitman's *Leaves Of Grass* one hundred years before. Labatt's brewery was invited to share the publicity by providing the beer for the party. Publicity was the name of the game.

Nancy and Merrill were back at Bon Echo and issued invitations to any and all who might further the cause. Headed "Salut au Monde" and measuring 8 1/2" x 22", the invitation outlines the history of Bon Echo and lists the programme speakers:

Mr. Merrill Denison

Dr. Frank Stiling, Vice-President, The University of Western Ontario, President of the Canadian Authors' Association.

Dr. E. J. Pratt. "Whitman the Poet."

Dr. Algernon D. Black, Leader of the New York Ethical Culture Society. "The Democratic Ideals of Walt Whitman."

Mr. A. E. McBride, President of the Grolier Society of Canada Limited. "A Milestone in Canadian Culture."

Mr. John Fisher of the Canadian Broadcasting Corporation.

The well-planned afternoon proceedings went off very well. The Grolier Society, in the person of Barry Holloway, hosted the buffet lunch prepared by Ted Courneya, who had previously scored such a hit with his sand-baked beans. Over one hundred and fifty guests milled around the point of land dividing the lower and upper Mazinaw and around the White House where Mike Schwager had the cold beer on ice.

In *The Tweed News* Sam Curry reported that part of the proceedings were to be broadcast over the Trans Canada network of the CBC. Gaining the most publicity, of course, was John Fisher, the CBC commentator, who had ended his speech by saying, "I hope Bon Echo will become a breeding ground for ideas in Canadian intellectual and cultural life." Although the story didn't hit the front page of *The Globe and Mail*, it was picked up by many dailies and weeklies in Eastern Ontario and was thus considered a success.

When the CAA buses had departed and other guests had thinned out, I discovered that the overnight guests Merrill had invited to stay outnumbered the beds available. That was typical of Merrill. He generously issued invitations to new friends as well as old ones without a thought about how we'd feed them or where they'd sleep. Luckily, I'd had Clara Wood there to baby-sit John Merrill so it fell to her, under Nancy's direction, to prepare dinner. John, myself and the children gave up our bedrooms to the overflow guests and went home for the night.

The festivities went on in Dollywood for another day or so.

Wally and Betty Floody with their two sons, Brian and Richard, 1955.

Two of the company were Solange and Yousuf Karsh. Merrill and Yousuf were old friends dating back to the days when Yousuf, an ambitious but far from wealthy immigrant from Armenia, had taken Merrill's advice and used just his last name when he began his career as a portrait photographer. One of his gifts to Muriel and Merrill had been the Irish terrier, Mister Boo. Polite and precise, Yousuf seemed not to be fond of the backwoods, so it was a surprise when he asked John to take him fishing. Our ten-year old daughter, Janet, went with them in the boat and John rowed out toward the Rock. Solange protested. Her husband knew nothing about boats. He surely would drown. In fact, Solange was unhappy the entire visit. She complained that the elevation was causing her severe distress. Never, before or since, have I ever heard anyone else make such a complaint. In due time, the fishermen returned with one small fish. I don't remember who caught it, but Yousuf was happy.

Nancy Palmer's two daughters were at Bon Echo, too. The elder was Martitia, known as Tish, a thin, dark, intense fourteen-year old. Nancy Lee, a year or so younger, was a sociable, easy-going kid. She and Janet became friends. Nancy was planning her elder daughter's future career as a movie star. She had engineered an audition in New York for Tish with no less than Otto Preminger, who was casting *Bon Jour Tristesse*. To that end Tish must learn to smoke. Nancy didn't smoke, but I did, so I was asked to offer the youngster a cigarette, usually after dinner, show her how to hold it, light it and how to avoid choking or appearing ill at ease. Although Tish failed to land a part in Preminger's movie, she did eventually make a name for herself in film, stage and TV performances in Rome, London and the United States. By 1982 she was a co-host on Boston's WCVB-TV's *Good Morning* show.

Overlapping and intertwined with the group in Dollywood were Jack Peterson's friends, three couples and several children, who were booked for Greystones on the 1st of July, but they came the day before. This caused quite a kerfuffel, but all were good-natured and cheerful, except Nancy. The Holloways, taking Clara with them to cook, moved over to the White House. This left a very displeased Nancy to cope with the crowd in Dollywood. The Holloways were not fond of Nancy, with good reason, as it turned out. She had already questioned Merrill about my position in the scheme of things. Why was I collecting cottage rent, even from him? She was beginning to realize she hadn't hooked such a big fish after all.

Among Jack Peterson's friends were Betty and Wally Floody with their sons, Brian and Richard. Wally, ex-RCAF Bomber Command, was the World War Two prisoner-of-war who had become famous as the man who engineered the tunnelling under the noses of German guards and whose story was told in *The Great Escape*. Betty's sister, Peggy, and her husband, Norman Armstrong, were there with their young son we knew as Cupcake. The three Stooges, as I called Namerow, Hunt and Pascal, who had painted the letters of Old Walt's inscription, were back for a week in the Goggin cabin. Again, there wasn't room for me and the children, so we were at home for a day or so until we could get back into Dollywood.

With mock-military precision, Jack Peterson had spent weeks planning what he called Exercise Bon Echo:

"OPERATION ORDER 'A'
INFORMATION
1. Enemy.
(a) Black flies and mosquitoes in appreciable strength, These formations have earned an enviable name in battle and are known as skillful, ruthless fighters. They may, however, be combatted to some degree by scientific preparations.
(b) Laziness - difficult to overcome
(c) Alcohol - impossible.
2. Our Troops.
(a) John Weir, geologist
(b) C. Wallace Floody, hard rock miner
(c) Colonel R. A. Keane, DSO, CBE, map reader
(d) J.F. Peterson, enthusiast
(e) John Savigny, local guide
(f) Mike Schwager, artist
(g) Joe Bonney, strategist
(h) Norman Armstong, humourist
(i) Merrill Denison, reporter
INTENTION
3. We shall capture the Pre-Cambrian Shield and establish the Good Friends' Mine. With more orders and instructions, the document was signed,
J. F. Peterson
Commander
Bon Echo Expeditionary Force 1955"

There *was* a serious aspect to this wacky operation, even though it was hard to detect. Maps had been recently published which showed magnetic anomalies in the local area which indicated the presence of huge amounts of iron ore. The most promising spots were on top of the Rock and some distance easterly, another was in the Vennachar area. The location Jack chose was Skootamatta Lake and land to the south. Each member of the expedition had obtained the necessary miner's licence and *Prospector's Guide* from the Department of Mines and Resources.

Reasonably early on Saturday morning, the 2nd of July, two boatloads of would-be claim stakers set off across Skootamatta

Lake. Merrill and Mike were not among them. John told me later that the whole effort was one hilarious fiasco. By lunch time they made landfall on a sandy beach in the upper lake. Eggs were strewn at the water's edge to keep them cool; some were hard-boiled and some were not. Whether the Colonel's army canteen full of whiskey was to blame, suffice to say that the Good Friends' Mine was staked on the beach. It was as big as the living room rug. But a good time was had by all, said John.

Back in Dollywood, I took up the reins again. Jane and Barry departed on the fifth and Clara came with me as cook-housekeeper and her teenage son, Wally Wood, was hired as chore boy to help Mike. Nancy, Merrill, Tish, Nancy Lee and Mister Boo left for Ottawa and Montreal where the history of the Bank of Montreal awaited the author. A short time later Nancy and Merrill left on a fifteen- hundred-mile motor trip to the east coast and visited a literary and recreational centre at Pugwash, Nova Scotia.

Just when I thought I had everything under control, Peggy and Norman Armstrong came to report they couldn't find the canoe they'd rented for the next week of their stay. We had only one canoe so its disappearance was of some concern to me. Mike eventually remembered that, before he left, Mr. Denison had given the three Stooges permission to take it off the property. Nobody thought to tell me of Merrill's generosity. At ten o'clock that evening, a wildly dishevelled, unshaven Pascal burst into Dollywood. He frightened Clara by opening the ice-box, demanding food. He frightened me, too. Clearly, he was in a dangerous mood. Chomping on cheese, or whatever he'd snatched from the ice-box, he announced they were leaving. Asked about the canoe, he said they would bring it back in a couple of weeks. Asked for the rent of five dollars a week, he said they had no money, but I could have whatever was left in the Goggin; some instant coffee and corn syrup. As soon as he left Dollywood I ran to Greystones to tell Peterson, Floody and Armstrong.

Those three stalwarts came to my aid immediately. After interviewing John Hunt and Richard Pascal in the Goggin, they advised me to call the police because Hunt and Pascal denied taking the canoe off the property. We never knew what had become of the third Stooge, Norman Namerow. Another man, however, was in the cabin. He was Wilfred Lessard, an old prospector who lived in the nearby village of Flinton. While waiting for the OPP constable to arrive, Floody and Armstrong stood guard at the back and terrace doors of Dollywood and Peterson kept watch on the Goggin cabin. I was truly thankful for the presence of those three impressive figures.

The constable rounded everyone up and brought them into the living room in Dollywood. Pascal confessed the canoe had been left up on poles on the shore of Partridge Lake. Lessard promised to bring it back by sundown the next day. I'm sure of all these details because I made a written report for Merrill. The canoe was returned in good condition. Not so the Goggin; it was filthy. We were all of the opinion that Hunt and Pascal, with or without Namerow, had got wind of the magnetometer survey and the iron ore deposits and had enlisted Lessard's aid to stake claims. Unfamiliar with the bush, they'd stayed out too long and run out of food, but why had Lessard allowed that to happen?

The Reverend Canon and Mrs. Stanley Andrews of Montreal were the next guests in the Goggin cabin. They had no previous association with Merrill or Bon Echo. I told Mrs. Andrews something about the previous occupants and showed her John Hunt's business card, "John Joseph Hunt, Reg'd. Aptitude Testing. Juvenile Delinquent Consultant." To my absolute astonishment, she told me she was Hunt's parole officer. Nancy Palmer, I decided, had some strange friends.

The rest of the season passed in relative peace and quiet. The couple who had honeymooned at Bon Echo in 1927 came again. Martha and Donald Camfield brought Martha's sister, husband and son, Humphrey. Arriving the first week of July they stayed until Labour Day. They hadn't intended such a long stay but, because of a polio epidemic in the sister's home town in up-state New York, they did not wish to return and so expose Humphrey to the risk. After the first reserved month they cheerfully accepted whatever accommodation I could offer and spent the last weeks in the Manager's House and two log sleeping cabins. They didn't even complain about the bucket they had in one of the cabins to catch the drips when it rained. I still have Martha's sketch of the Mazinaw which she gave to me.

These memories of forty years ago include the morning Clara
had such a fright. On rare occasions, Merrill chose to enjoy the
Mazinaw in the quiet of the early morning. His routine was to
don his yellow swim trunks with the painting of the Rock on the
seat. Among his friends, those were famous swim trunks, old but
still in good shape. The painting of the Rock was still clear and
bright, painted years before by a lady whose name, I think, was
Bowie. Usually, Merrill walked slowly into the lake until he was
chest-deep, then rolled onto his back, there to float motionless
and contemplate the sky. Glancing out of Dollywood's kitchen
window, Clara saw him thus. She rushed upstairs to my bedroom
moaning, "Mr. Denison's dead in the water!"

A very happy memory is of Merrill's friend, Eugene Kash,
known as Jack. He was a symphony orchestra violinist of some
note and husband of the famous Canadian singer, Maureen
Forrester. He brought his violin. I remember Greystones' living
room being filled with guests and a child sitting on each step of
the staircase, face peering out through the balustrade. Jack
entranced us all. He played well-known classics, show tunes, folk
songs, hymns, even nursery rhymes and brought a lump to every
grown-up throat when he played "Danny Boy." Jack told us his
violin was insured for four thousand dollars, which we thought a
vast sum. The combination of the fine instrument and such a tal-
ented musician made a memory to last a lifetime.

In Dollywood, one afternoon later in the season, Merrill complained of weakness, chest pain and breathing difficulty. I guided
him to the couch in front of the fire and covered him with a blan-
ket. He refused to allow me to push the panic button, just wanted
to rest for a while. It struck me as very odd that, although Nancy
was in the room, he appealed to me for help. Nancy looked on for
a few minutes then retired to her bedroom. A day or so later, John
took Merrill to Tweed to consult with Dr. Frank McCue, our G.P.
He opined that Merrill's heart and lungs were not in the best condition, but the patient was feeling better by then and resumed his
busy schedule.

Meanwhile, Jack Peterson was trying to hold the Bon Echo
Committee together. The Bon Echo Foundation was composed of
men who were the figure heads of the organization. The Bon

Echo Committee members were the actual working body. On the 7th September, 1955, the first committee meeting was held at the Château Laurier Hotel in Ottawa, in the suite of Hugh A. Mackenzie, Executive Vice President of John Labatt Limited. Reading the minutes of that meeting it is clear that trouble was ahead. Mr. Gordon Cushing, of the Trades and Labour Congress, explained that his and his union's priority was Club Whitesands, a recreation and conference centre forty miles north of Peterborough, Ontario, on Lake Catchacoma. The International Chemical Workers' Union had spent a lot of money there. It was unlikely that funds would be available for Bon Echo.

Mr. W. B. Greenwood, Chief of the Division of Parks, Department of Lands and Forests, Queen's Park, naturally saw things from the department point of view. He said he was willing to cooperate with the committee, seemingly forgetting that he was a member of the committee, but it was not possible to conduct a physical survey of the property, or otherwise invest, so long as it was privately owned. The only enthusiastic committee members, as far as I could see, were Dr. Roby Kidd of the Canadian Association for Adult Education and his brother, John Kidd of the Canadian Citizenship Council. Merrill had his doubts, though he didn't voice them.

With no visible means of support, Nancy continued as Merrill's companion. She sought employment in Philadelphia with Adlai Stevenson's presidential campaign committee. Nancy and Merrill had met with the democratic party's candidate earlier when a speaker for the Canadian Authors' Association was being sought. Stevenson did not come to Bon Echo and he didn't employ Nancy. Using her considerable linguistic talents, she also aimed to organize the Round the World Study Tour of the Putney Graduate School, so Merrill told me. It was in his 22nd December letter to John and me that he told of a meeting which held the key to his future. From Washington, D.C., he wrote:

> "We [Nancy, Martitia, Nancy Lee and Merrill] drove from New York here yesterday. Washington is a marvellous city at night and Lisa Andrews, whom we are visiting, had a most cheery welcome for us. John [Lisa's son] is taking Martitia to her first dance tonight and everyone is most excited about it."

6
A Gift to the People of Ontario

A T CHRISTMAS, 1955, Elizabeth Robert Andrews, known as Lisa, was recently divorced and with son, John, lived in a prestigious area of Georgetown, Washington, D.C. There Merrill enjoyed the best Christmas he'd known in years. It didn't take him long to discover that he and Nancy's friend shared a great deal in common, both professionally and personally. Their friendship blossomed. Perhaps Nancy planned it that way.

Nancy and Merrill were together in Montreal in March, 1956. Nancy was still hopeful that a job could be found for her with the Adlai Stevenson presidential campaign committee and Merrill wanted the girls to spend some time at Bon Echo before they went off to Formosa to be with their father, a U.S. Army officer. But we never saw the Palmer family again. We heard that Nancy had left for Rome, Italy.

Early in 1956 I was feeling unwell with some undiagnosed ailment and had to advise Merrill that I could continue to handle his manuscripts, but managing Bon Echo was beyond my strength. Typically, Merrill tried to help. We should get ourselves to Montreal where we could borrow Bundles, the 1940 Ford convertible, proceed to the Holloways in New Rochelle, who would be happy to accommodate us and I could get "a dependable diagnosis from the famous Dr. Howard Rusk, one of the Holloways' best friends." All easier said than done. We stayed home with our three children, our dog Sally and Mister Boo, who had been with us all winter and would stay until Merrill returned to Bon Echo in the spring. A thyroid disorder was diagnosed, but that was years later.

The summer seasons of 1956 and 1957 were quiet at Bon Echo. Jack Peterson rented Greystones again. I was there with family and friends from time to time, often with Jane and Barry Holloway. Merrill came whenever he could be sure someone would be there to cook his meals. If alone at lunch time, he made his favorite sandwich; a thick slice of Bermuda onion between two slices of bread, with a bottle of beer to wash it down. Merrill's most important guest of the summer of 1956 was, of course, his new friend, Lisa Andrews, who brought along her eighteen-year old son, John. Lisa was eight years younger than Merrill, interested in him and his work, his hopes for Bon Echo and was fun to be with. Her voice was low and husky and I used to tell her she sounded just like Tallulah Bankhead. She and I got along famously, in part because we appreciated each other's quirky sense of humour.

On the 12th March, 1957, Merrill signed a seven-page agreement with John Labatt Limited, which sets out the plan for all the Bon Echo property. Part would be developed by the Bon Echo Committee as a conference centre, the "meeting place," the bulk of the estate would be turned over to the Department of Lands and Forests, to be known as Labatt Provincial Park. The three main cottages, with a small acreage, would remain for Merrill's use, free of dower, until his death when that also would become part of the Bon Echo Foundation property. Labatts agreed to continue to bear the committee's expenses, which included Mike's wages and the township taxes, in an amount not to exceed five thousand dollars. If they could not complete "the necessary arrangements" with the Department of Lands and Forests within six months, the agreement would be terminated.

Unfortunately, Jack Peterson became ill and faded from the picture. John Kidd, of the Canadian Citizenship Council, had camped at Bon Echo with his family and had published a lengthy report covering a wide range of topics including timber, water, sewage, parking and proposals for suitable buildings. John Kidd had high hopes and may have envisioned his own and his family's future at Labatt Provincial Park. Except for W. B. Greenwood, the Chief of the Division of Parks, who had his own schemes for Merrill's property becoming a provincial park, John Kidd, by that time, was the only member of the Bon Echo Foundation or the Bon Echo Committee who spent much time on the project.

The author, Mike Schwager and Pat Holloway, Jane and Barry's daughter-in-law, outside the White House, 1957.

In the summer of 1957 Merrill brought two more friends to Bon Echo. They were Vera and Peter Kurnicki, who looked after Merrill for a few weeks. One can still see Peter's contribution to Bon Echo. At one corner of the Dollywood dining porch is a cedar post carved in a spiral pattern. Peter asked my husband to find a suitable length of cedar and a telephone pole was obtained from James Vogan, of Northbrook, owner of the local telephone system. Peter was Polish, a senior man with the Montreal Parks Department. Vera was a blue-blooded Russian who, in the nick of time, had escaped with her family at the beginning of the 1917 Bolshevik Revolution. She remembered her sheltered early life and told of her nursemaid warming her shoes by blowing into them before putting them on her feet. Vera made good borscht.

Before the year was out, Lisa and Merrill were married quietly in Gloucester, Massachusetts. For the next couple of years Lisa realized she had also married Bon Echo, as had Muriel before her. It is from a bulky file of correspondence which Merrill gave to my husband for safe-keeping that the story can be traced. These letters are mainly between Merrill and his solicitor and longtime, patient friend, Leonard V. Sutton of Holmsted, Sutton, Hill & Kemp, Toronto. Merrill gave this file to John because he did not wish the contents to be available to the public during his lifetime, as they could have been had they gone with all his other papers to Queen's University, Kingston.

Early in 1958 the Anglican Bishop of the Diocese of Ontario, the Right Reverend Kenneth Evans, was in communication with the Denisons. The Reverend Earle Hawkes, then Rector of the Parish of Tweed and North Addington Mission, and the Reverend Desmond Hunt, on the bishop's behalf, met with them to discuss the possibility of Bon Echo becoming an Anglican Church conference centre. Merrill was strenuously opposed and would only consider such a development if all denominations, colours, creeds and races were included. However, he admitted that because Lisa was in favour and his first wife, Muriel, and her father, Dr. David Goggin, had been such pillars of the Anglican Church, he would give the church's proposals every consideration. In a short time Bishop Evans had to concede that the project was too vast and, in any event, funding was not available.

The Labatt agreement having expired, Merrill turned to the Province of Ontario as the only means of keeping Bon Echo intact. On the 13th May, 1958, Leonard Sutton opened the negotiations on behalf of Lisa and Merrill by writing a letter to W. B. Greenwood, Department of Lands and Forests. All the property was offered at that time, except Merrill reserved a life interest in Dollywood, Greystones and the Cement House. "In return for a conveyance of Bon Echo to the province Mr. Denison would expect the province to pay him $12,000 to take care of the present encumbrances and some other items," said Mr. Sutton.

There were long-standing mortgages and loans which Merrill had never been able to discharge. Years ago he had borrowed money from Harry Levere of Cloyne. Harry was allowed to cut timber as part repayment but two mortgages were still outstanding, amounting to almost $3,000. Mr. Holmsted, Leonard Sutton's senior law partner, held a mortgage of $1,000. The Fiduciary Trust Company of Boston was owed $2,500. That sum had been secured

Two Merrills in Dollywood, 1958.

John Merrill, Lisa and Mister Boo in Dollywood, 1958.

since the twenties by Donald Moffat, the good friend Merrill made during World War One when they served together on an American ambulance crew. A man called Carl Pike of Boston had loaned Merrill $1,000. The unpaid solicitor's account was over $1,500 and even the Tweed branch of the Bank of Montreal held a note for $300, which amount Merrill had borrowed to buy "refreshments" for the Bon Echo Foundation party in 1955. This indebtedness was the main reason, though there were others, that the province did not acquire Bon Echo until 1959.

Following Merrill's offer of the 13th May, 1958, the province, in the person of W. Benny Greenwood, a member of both the Bon Echo Foundation and its working committee, advised that the gift possibly could be accepted but, first, the loans and mortgages against the property must be discharged. John Kidd apparently was not told of this offer to the province. He was still presuming that his and the Labatt plans were ongoing, though that agreement had expired in September, 1957. Understandably, his reaction and that of several other members of the Bon Echo Committee was "shock and disappointment." His letters to Merrill are not in the file, but a letter from Lisa to Leonard Sutton describes them as "almost libelous, certainly malicious and impertinent."

Before accepting the gift, the province's solicitor, Mr. Yoerger, also required releases from John Labatt Limited and from the Bon Echo Committee. Another stumbling block was the fact that a neighbour to the south, James Main, had encroached unwittingly onto Merrill's land when he built his cottage. That required a survey, description, deed and more legal aid. Lisa and Merrill, for their part, wanted assurance that the property would be developed for "the purpose of conservation, education and recreation," but the province could not make such assurances. Merrill remarked, "Quetico and Algonquin are one thing, Wasaga Beach is another." Lisa imagined tents and trailers on the north beach which would certainly spoil their enjoyment of the property.

Meanwhile, ever willing to take on more work, Merrill had embarked on another "pot boiler." This was the history of Ontario Hydro, *The People's Power*. Work was also progressing on the Bank of Montreal book, though slowly. Researchers were sending data which had to be entered on the big sheets of paper I've previously described. Merrill had a writing assistant, a bright young Englishman named Guy Meyler, who was installed in Dollywood. Even so, Merrill was falling behind with his work. Both he and Lisa were becoming increasingly frustrated and angry with the way provincial representatives were delaying acceptance of the gift of Bon Echo. In the file which Merrill gave to my husband, there are over fifty letters written during 1958 to and from Merrill and his solicitor, Leonard Sutton, all having to do with these negotiations. Unable to give his full attention to his work, Merrill told Leonard Sutton that he was "facing professional disaster."

A visit from the County Assessor in July, 1958, gave Merrill some idea of the worth of his property. At $10 per foot for the rocky shoreline and $15 per foot for the sand beaches, he estimated he was giving the province the equivalent of $200,000, and they were quibbling about $12,000.

It was about this time that John, my husband, realized that if Merrill gave away all his land he would soon find his financial security in jeopardy. He told Lisa of his concern and she agreed. Together, they appealed to Merrill to re-think. After two or three evenings of discussion they were successful in persuading him to retain shoreline to the north and the south. Far removed from the core of the property, this land could be developed for commercial and cottage use and thus produce additional income when required. For those readers with township map in hand, the parcels retained were Lots 34, 35 and 40 in the 2nd Range and small parts of Lots 43 and 44 east of Highway 41 in Range B, in Barrie Township, Frontenac County. In total, the area was less than one hundred acres.

Of course, it was impossible for Merrill to beg, borrow, steal or even earn enough money to pay out his loans and mortgages and so satisfy Mr. Yoerger, the province's solicitor. He did, however, confide to Leonard Sutton that maybe Lisa could provide the funds. She had sold her house in Washington, but she wisely declined to share the proceeds. Throughout the fall and winter of 1958 Leonard Sutton laboured on his client's behalf. Finally, the province agreed to allow Merrill $12,000 as "compensation" in return for the deed which would transfer Bon Echo to Her Majesty the Queen in the Right of the Province of Ontario. The total acreage was in excess of twelve hundred acres.

It must have been with a huge sigh of relief that Leonard Sutton signed his five-page letter to Merrill, dated 2nd March, 1959, which begins, "We are pleased to report that the transfer to the Province of Ontario has been completed." All the registered creditors had been reimbursed and Merrill received a cheque for $4,955.20 to cover other outstanding indebtedness. No trumpets, no fanfare, no news releases. Merrill would have to wait a few years for formal recognition of his gift to the People of Ontario.

Elizabeth Robert Denison with the pigeons in Trafalgar Square, 1959.

"Beyond belief!" said he, "I've just realized we're the Queen's tenants."

The summer of 1959 should have brought little change to the Denisons' life at Bon Echo. Mike was assured of his wages, having been put on the Department of Lands and Forests' payroll, as had Harry Levere. Merrill and Guy Meyler resumed work in earnest. I was spending long hours at the "tripewriter" which, to Merrill's amusement, was his young godson's pronunciation. "Out of the mouths of babes," he said. Lisa was spending time improving her surroundings in Greystones, which was the cottage she preferred. There were new curtains and cushion covers, even new windows in the living room. To take care of the cooking and clening, Lisa brought two capable Afro-Canadian women from Montreal. I knew them as Betty and Marlene and they lived in the Cement House where, according to long-established custom, they served the meals.

A few months previously we had moved from the old farmhouse south of Northbrook to an even older log house at Story Lake, near Cloyne. Presently owned by Gwen and Blake Lloyd, it is purported to be the oldest inhabited dwelling in Barrie Township. It was there, about two or three o'clock in the morning, that Merrill phoned to say that the Cement House was on fire and please could John do something about it. While John threw on some clothes, I phoned Harry Levere in Cloyne and he was ready to go when John arrived at his house. There was no fire fighting equipment in the area except that which belonged to the Department of Lands and Forests stored at the Slow Boys' Camp, north of Bon Echo. We knew the forestry camp by that name because the sign on Highway 41 read, "Slow—Boys' Camp." With no traffic at that hour, John broke the speed limit in his army station wagon. Harry, having the key to the camp building, found the water pump and hose, and he and John loaded them into the wagon.

Arriving at the fire, the men carefully set up the pump on the beach in front of the blazing Cement House and ran out the hose, only to find that the engine was seized. Harry called the department at Plevna and eventually, soon after dawn, help arrived, but all they could do was soak the embers. The Cement House was reduced to ashes.

Betty and Marlene had been sleeping upstairs. They had had a fire in the living room fireplace and apparently the cement in the old stone chimney had fallen away allowing fire to escape to the wooden rafters. The women fled in terror to Greystones to awaken Merrill. Lisa tried to calm them. They were losing their possessions. A few weeks earlier Lisa had been concerned about Betty, who was still suffering the effects of back surgery, and she had paid all of sixty dollars for a custom-fitted corset. Commiserating with Betty about the loss of all her clothing, especially her new corset which was so much appreciated, Lisa was surprised to hear Betty say, "Miss Denison, I didn't lose my new corset. I never take it off."

The Cement House had been a two-storey frame structure, enlarged since Flora's time and stuccoed with cement, thus the name. Other than Mike's cottage, it was the only building that could be used in winter and was believed to have been the first which Dr. Price built. John personally complained to the department about the condition of their equipment and their excuse was "that is no longer a fire location" and the pump was "redundant."

Lost in the fire were the finer pieces of china, glassware and silver which Flora, and especially Muriel, had collected over the years. They had been stored in a huge two-door cupboard. A particular loss to Merrill was his wind-up gramophone and his collection of 78 rpm records, including half a dozen recordings of *The Red Army Sings*. Not by any standards could Merrill be described as musical, but there were a couple of songs he really enjoyed. They were "Never On A Sunday" and the one about the "Itsy Bitsy Teeny Weeny Yellow Polka Dot Bikini." A year or so after the fire, John planted a kitchen garden for Lisa and four red rose bushes, one at each corner of the place where the Cement House once stood. If one looks carefully, they can still be found, especially in summer when the red roses are blooming.

Casting about for additional funds, Merrill realized he still held title to Big Bear Island in the Upper Mazinaw. He and John put their heads together and decided John should attempt to sell it. A classified ad in *The Globe And Mail* brought forth a buyer who agreed to pay the asking price of $2,200. John composed an agreement of purchase and sale, with copies for all concerned, accepted a deposit and sent Leonard Sutton a copy of the agreement in order that he could prepare the deed. Mr. Sutton's junior partner, Linton W. Scott, was quick to inform Merrill that, although the sale would be completed, he should advise Mr. Savigny that he was contravening the law inasmuch as it was illegal to attempt to sell real estate on behalf of another party without a licence so to do. That news was responsible for a dramatic change in our lives.

John determined that becoming a real estate broker would be a sound idea. In 1959 it was not nearly so difficult as it is today. From the Department of Consumer and Commercial Affairs John received a potted version of the Real Estate Act, was allowed two weeks to memorize the contents and then went to Perth to the sheriff's office to write an examination. He passed the examination and became a real estate broker. That's all there was to it. John's appliance store by then was in Northbrook. Formerly, it had been a dance hall, so there was lots of room to include the new business. Savigny Real Estate Limited is still in business today, with David and his wife, Karen, as brokers.

Next year, encouraged by this turn of events, Merrill agreed to allow John to develop his most northerly Mazinaw shoreline, known then as Hurricane Strip for obvious reasons. The storm's devastation was then still apparent, though it was caused by a tornado, not a hurricane. Surveyed and divided into lots, access roads and driveways were bulldozed. Storm-damaged trees and trees uprooted by the bulldozer littered the landscape. At this rough stage in the development, Merrill decided to go and see what was going on. Barry O'Dwyer drove him there. Barry was the new writing assistant and learning to drive. He reported to us that Merrill was shocked by what he saw and could not believe that anyone would be interested in buying.

The most northerly lots were too narrow for cottage construction, but were ideal boathouse lots for people whose cottages were without road access on the other side of the lake. The rest of the lots were rough and rocky, but all have magnificent views of the upper lake and the northern end of the Rock. With a couple of dozen other properties to sell, newsprint flyers were printed by *The Tweed News*. In a short time John had an offer to purchase to present to Merrill. He was amazed and, as usual, pronounced that it was "beyond belief," and happily affixed his signature. Barry was equally jubilant and pleased that John had made a sale. "Nothing succeeds like success," he said, and that is still our oft-quoted maxim.

Merrill's gift to the province had given rise to complaints from some township residents that their property taxes were bound to rise because so much land had reverted to the Crown and thus struck from the tax rolls. Resort owners complained that the new Bon Echo Provincial Park would be in direct competition with their establishments. To offset these complaints was the fact that many local people found employment at Bon Echo. As well, over the next few years Merrill sold twenty-five lakeshore lots which my husband, John Savigny, had developed. The cottages and homes built more than compensated for the township's initial tax loss.

Godson Merrill on the North Beach, 1960.

Resort owners had no reason to fear. Their clientele was a different breed from the campers at the park. More importantly, the advertising and interest generated by the park led to many more vacationers becoming aware of the Land 0' Lakes area of Eastern Ontario. Thousands of people have visited, and will visit, the park and their contribution to local business is beyond calculation.

Gerald McMurray, from Gilmour, was the first superintendent at the park. He was patient with Lisa, as were succeeding superintendents, Wayne Miller and Edward Buck. She was apt to be a nuisance with her continual requests for this and that. The woodhouse behind Greystones needed repair, the back steps, too, and the blackflies and/or mosquitoes should be sprayed and so on, and on. Neither Lisa or Merrill had reason to complain about the way the park was developed. Every care was taken to ensure that there was no unnecessary tree-felling or camp sites situated within their sight. Swimming was not allowed on the north beach because the water intake was still in use there. When we drove up in the evening we had to stop at the gatehouse and say, "We're visiting the Denisons." Often we caught a whiff of the campers' hamburgers being cooked, but otherwise we hardly knew we were in a provincial park. If Merrill could see the place now I'm sure he would approve.

With *The People's Power* successfully published in 1960, Merrill gave attention to the Bank of Montreal history. Following Barry O'Dwyer as writing assistant came Mickey Huband, a bank employee, and Mike Addinall. Mike and his wife, Tina, became good friends of the Denisons. Mike was more than a writing assistant. He supported Merrill in many personal ways above and beyond the call of duty. More than anyone else, he understood Merrill's years of painstaking work and the pressure he experienced when bank officials enquired about the book's completion date. Mike was a sympathetic listener to all the problems of the day. He helped sort out the bank balances and the bills needing payment. He chauffeured Merrill hither and yon. He was a trusted companion and I know he enjoyed the good times they had together. The Addinalls' enduring link with Bon Echo is their summer home, not very far north of the park boundary.

At long last, in 1964, Greystones and Dollywood were wired for electricity. Lisa went on a shopping spree, buying electrical gadgets, especially lamps and lampshades suitable for the cottages' decor. To celebrate the event, the Denisons hosted a "lighting-up" party, a thank-you to the department officials. From Tweed the District Forester, Jim Taylor, came with his wife, Jean. The Tweed District Supervisor of Parks, Harold Cantelon, was there with his wife, Ruth. The park superintendent, Gerald McMurray, came with his wife, Marcie, and other members of the park staff, including Mike Schwager. Lizzie and Harry Levere were there from Cloyne. The surprise was that Merrill also invited Lois and Lionel Jamieson with their square-dance team from Kaladar. Lionel was the village postmaster and Lois taught at the Flinton public school. Merrill was not the least bit interested in dancing of any kind, but he probably decided square-dancing was better than having the group sitting around looking at each other and the new lamps. In Dollywood's living room, with the rugs rolled up and the furniture pushed against the walls, the party was a huge success, going on until the wee hours of the morning.

Two special events marked 1965. Merrill completed the final manuscript of the first volume of *Canada's First Bank, A History of the Bank of Montreal*. It was published in 1966 and received satisfying reviews. After all those long years of work which produced 471 pages, Merrill could rest more easily, though only momentarily. Volume Two, equally weighty, was still to be finished, though it and the French translation took only little more than a year.

Merrill's long-awaited day was the 21st of July. At last the fanfare, the trumpets and the news releases. Kilted pipers of the Lanark and Renfrew Scottish Regiment led the official party to the amphitheatre where the opening ceremonies took place. The Department of Lands and Forests staged a fitting ceremony to mark his sustained, but often frustrated, dedication to his mother's intention to keep Bon Echo intact. Forty-four years after Merrill accepted his inheritance, he received formal acknowledgement of his gift to the People of Ontario. On that lovely summer day, Lisa and Merrill unveiled the plaque fixed to a huge boulder, close by the narrows, which reads:

ACQUIRED BY
THE PEOPLE OF ONTARIO
THROUGH THE GENEROSITY OF
MR. AND MRS. MERRILL DENISON
BON ECHO PROVINCIAL PARK
DEDICATED TO
RECREATION, CONSERVATION AND EDUCATION
IN MEMORY OF
FLORA MacDONALD DENISON
AND
MURIEL GOGGIN DENISON
DEPARTMENT OF LANDS & FORESTS
Hon. A. Kelso Roberts, Q.C., Minister
F. A. MacDougall, Deputy Minister
July 21, 1965

Memorial plaque, 1965.

7
The Closing Years

B Y THE SUMMER OF 1965 the White House had been demolished and, at Lisa's request, the Manager's House was taken apart log by log to be re-erected up the hill beyond Greystones, close to Sawmill Bay and re-named the Cabin on the Hill. This was the second time the building had been re-located. Merrill told us that it was the original one-room school in the French Settlement in which his mother had taught, eighty years before. The bottom logs had to be replaced and Gerald McMurray, the park superintendent, turned for help from my husband, John, who was at that time co-chairman of the Centennial Committee of Barrie Township.

In anticipation of Canada's one-hundredth birthday in 1967, a few local residents, including our good friends, Barbara and John Lester, planned building a log museum in Cloyne on township land beside Benny's Lake. The Lesters were among the newer full-time Mazinaw residents, having bought a small acreage at the foot of the lake in 1961, where they established a successful marina. Barbara, from Sarnia and John, from Toronto, had met years previously at Whip-Poor-Will Lodge at the northern end of the lake. John was a member of an Ontario Hydro crew then surveying the transmission line that crosses Highway 41 between Mazinaw and Mackavoy lakes, on its route from Stewartsville and Barrett Chute to Oshawa. Barbara was vacationing with her sister, Nadine Brumell, her brother-in-law, Ralph and two nephews, Ian and Tony. Soon after marriage they bought shoreline on the east side of the lake from the Crown and built a log cabin to which they escaped when they weren't in some remote Hydro camp. When they had saved enough money, John left Ontario Hydro and they were able to realize their dream of living and working year round beside the lake they loved.

John A. Lester 1924–1994.

Barbara Lester 1920–1994.

Nadine Brumell, Cloyne, 1979.

Both enthusiastic supporters of the community in many ways, they joined with us in the plan to erect a small, log building in which to preserve and display artifacts and memorabilia of the early settlers of the district. Highway 41 was then being improved and the log home of Ada and Percy Levere was in the way of progress. The Centennial Committee members had permission to use those squared logs to build their museum. However, loud complaints were heard from the lady who lived next door to the museum site. "We've been working and slaving for years to get out of log cabins. I don't want to see another one. Don't bring those logs here!" So, the project was shelved. Eventually, the Pioneer Museum was built but not with the Levere logs, they had to be sawn for the purpose.

Those Levere logs, we discovered, had originally come from the Skootamatta Lake Road where some had been boom logs and been part of a lumber company cookhouse used by the log drivers. Some of those logs are now the underpinnings of a log cottage we built on Shabomeka Lake. At least one of the boom logs, identified by the company's initial hammered into them and the holes through which chains linked them together, can be seen among the bottom logs of the Cabin on the Hill. Lisa made a cosy get-away for herself. Most of the cabin is sitting room for which she bought a luxurious leather couch and other accoutrements. There's a small bedroom and a tiny bathroom.

Greystones has a long history, too. Lisa's bedroom on the north and Merrill's bedroom on the south, together with the living room, are now part of the park's gift shop although new partitions tend to hide the original structure. The living room is log and came from the east end of Campbell Bay in the Upper Mazinaw, so Merrill said. It was a school house especially built for a family with umpteen children. The story goes that one teacher after another was sent over there to educate those children, but life with that isolated family was intolerable and they all escaped. So eventually, Flora had the log building brought across the lake to become part of Greystones.

My husband and I introduced Merrill to Barbara and John Lester and he was happy to find they were not only fond of the Mazinaw, but were knowledgeable about the history of the area and equally concerned about its conservation. Like Merrill, they were not hunters or even anglers, though they owned Lester Marina. Talking to them and their customers, Merrill was becoming aware that the Mazinaw he knew was changing. Crown lots were being sold and, on his own lots, cottages and year round homes were being built. Dollywood and Greystones had long been the most elaborate on the lake, but he was amazed to find cottages being built which offered much more in modern convenience and comfort.

He was fascinated to see how the whole area was developing. He once remarked upon the difference power lawn mowers had made around the homes he saw as he drove up Highway 41. Until the mid-fifties, Merrill was rarely disturbed by high-powered motor boats put-putting through the narrows and then roaring off up the lake. The only motor boat to arrive at Bon Echo belonged to Gracie and Bob Wiren. Gracie was Merrill's cousin and daughter of Judge William H. Merrill, Flora's brother. They owned an ancient cottage on the lower lake, near the cottage which Flora had owned in the early 1900's.

Merrill came to know Barbara Lester's sister, Nadine Brumell,

whose family had long been Mazinaw cottagers, though Merrill
had no knowledge of that fact. He was delighted to learn that
they shared a common interest in geology, even though Nadine
had a much deeper understanding of the subject than he had. For
so many years, insulated in the fastness of Bon Echo, it just did-
n't occur to Merrill that anything interesting was going on
beyond his own boundaries.

Complaining to Barbara one day about the long drive to Tweed
for supplies, he told her he'd just made the trip in pouring rain.
All the way there, he said, his windshield wipers were saying,
"Liquor store, liquor store, liquor store!" Not many months later,
the Liquor Control Board of Ontario set up shop in part of the
Legion Hall in Northbrook. Barbara wrote this:

THE BALLAD OF NORTHBROOK BOOZE

It was in our Northern Spaces
That the feuding, founding races
Used to suffer in extremis
Due to isolation blues.
Not the fear of illness haunted,
Nor of lonely childbirth daunted,
But the dreadful possibility
Of running out of booze.

There were drastic measures taken
By those suffering souls forsaken
To achieve a decent surcease
Of their ever-present need.
In the hills the stills were stewing,
Every kitchen was a-brewing,
For the nearest legal outlet
Lay far off in distant Tweed.

But insidious civilization
Crept upon this northern nation,
And by the year Centennial
There were cops in every tree.
Old still keepers bent and wizened

Were dismantled or imprisoned
And the state of desperation
Grew most pitiful to see.

But their Fates did not forget them
As their dreadful thirst beset them,
Built a booze house right in Northbrook,
(So their grace all men may know)
Filled it with the finest liquor,
Now they get drunk all the quicker
Singing Glory Halleluja!
In their own L.C.B.O.

Written for Merrill Denison.

The park staff brought the natural amphitheatre at Bon Echo into use. A building was erected with a small stage and big logs sliced in half were installed as seating, creating an outdoor theatre accommodating an audience of five or six hundred. Several members of the Anglican Parish of Land O' Lakes, in particular those attending St. John's Church in Cloyne, saw an opportunity to provide interdenominational worship services for the hundreds of campers at the park. Though Merrill no longer had any control over happenings in the park, it seemed only courteous to tell him of the church's hope to conduct Sunday services and seek his opinion. As expected, he was not enthusiastic, but remembered his response in 1958 to Bishop Evans when that reverend gentleman had plans to make Bon Echo an Anglican Church camp. If all are welcome then he wouldn't complain.

The Department of Lands and Forests granted permission though, quite reasonably, they laid down the ground rules. The worship services were to be just that. No altar calls. Nothing to be offered for sale, such as tracts, books, records or trinkets. The advertising posters were vetted. Each week the chaplain was required to submit the order of service and the visiting preacher's name to the park superintendent. A park employee would unlock and lock the building behind the stage and count the congregation. With the blessing of our diocesan bishop, the Right Reverend Jack

Creeggan, and the services of an eager eighteen-year old Church Army cadet from Toronto, we advertised the Sunday morning services and the preliminary hymn-sing.

St. John's Church, where the Sunday congregation might number ten or twelve, was closed for the summer. The pump organ from St. John's was taken to Bon Echo with hymn booklets and collection tins. Chaplain Bill Ransom conducted the services and I played the pump organ. We were nervous that first Sunday morning in July, 1969, and as Bill gazed solemnly out at the sea of faces in the amphitheatre, I hissed at him from behind the organ, "Smile, darn you, smile!" He did, and his youthful enthusiasm was well received. That summer, up to 425 people were counted present at any one service. It was the largest congregation in the deanery, probably the whole diocese.

The unique congregation of the Cathedral in the Pines was comprised of as many as twenty-six different denominations. That was discovered because questionnaires were distributed in those days, but I don't remember whether or not that was a park rule. There was no dress rule. People came in shorts, some came with bare feet. They brought their babies in strollers and their dogs on leashes. They came by boat and, with special admission tickets to the park, they came from the local villages and summer resorts. Guest speakers were a special feature of the services and the committee was able to attract such notables as the Reverend Wilbur K. Howard, Moderator of the United Church and leaders of several other Christian denominations. As Barry O'Dwyer used to say, "Nothing succeeds like success."

One summer morning in 1969 a big cube van from Queen's University, Kingston, drove up to Bon Echo. Hours later it left, filled with two tons of "Denisonia." Merrill had sold the accumulated paper of years and almost all his books for $25,000. Boxes of manuscripts, letters, files and photographs were taken from closets and cupboards in both cottages and even from the storage shed where cleaning supplies and such were kept. The collection of books included a great many which had arrived in 1955 from the New York apartment and were arranged on wooden planks supported by bricks, all the way down the hall to Merrill's office in Dollywood.

The collection represents the work of his mother, Flora Mac-Donald Denison; his first wife, Muriel Goggin Denison; and the letters of Muriel's father, Dr. David Goggin and his own monumental mass of work. Queen's University Archivist and teacher in the history department, John A. Archer, wrote "The Merrill Denison Papers," a descriptive article published in the Autumn, 1969, edition of *Douglas Library Notes*. Therein he said:

"The Denison Papers are a rich, varied, interesting and extensive collection. They include manuscripts of published works, unpublished manuscripts, histories, radio scripts, fiction, serious articles, book reviews, letters, newspaper clippings—and a good library."

To sort and catalogue this enormous volume of paper was a gargantuan task for the university staff and it took a long time. This is such a varied collection that the interests of those seeking information must be just as varied.

With cash in hand from Queen's University and no major work to take his attention, Merrill was able to pursue matters of no less importance, but in a lighter vein. This is a letter he wrote on the 4th August, 1969:

"C. E. St. Germain, District Director
Canada Post Office, (Postes Canadiennes)
c/o Postmaster
Cloyne, Ontario
SUBJECT: CLOYNE R.R. No. 1
Your file 13-3-100 Cloyne R.R. No. 1
My file Literary Lapses No. 422

My dear Mr. District Director:
I have before me the above-mentioned mimeographed ukase directing me to remove from the said CLOYNE R.R. No. 1 one of the two mail boxes (installed there by me some years ago upon the insistence of the Post Office Department) or suffer dire consequences. I am impelled to ask you for a further explanation of the document above noted.

Just what do you mean, for example, when you refer to 'the right hand side of the road?' As you are no doubt aware,

Cloyne R.R. No. 1 services the King's Highway 41, which is a two-lane thoroughfare running in a northerly direction from the village of Cloyne to the village of Denbigh and in a southerly direction from the village of Denbigh to the aforesaid village of Cloyne.

Such being the circumstances, it is obvious that a mail box installed on the east side of Highway 41 would be on the right hand side of the road when the courier is proceeding in a northerly direction, but on the left hand side of the road when he is proceeding southward which I understand he is obliged to do in the pursuit of his daily rounds.

It is obvious that similar confusion would arise with respect to a mail box placed on the west side of the Highway, since it would be on the left hand side of the road to a courier proceeding north and on the right hand side of the road when he is headed south.

From which side of Highway 41, therefore, would you suggest that I remove one of my mail boxes? I might point out that this is fast becoming an academic question since the diversion of Highway 41 around the Bon Echo Provincial Park will shortly make both of my existing mailboxes redundant. Still, it would be nice to get the matter straightened out in principle.

This is a rather more important matter than may appear on the surface. If the courier, more properly the 'mail contractor,' is to deliver incoming mail and pick up outgoing mail from a box located on the east side of the Highway whilst proceeding northward, he would then have to transport the said outgoing mail with him to Denbigh before returning southward to deposit it in the Cloyne Post Office, whence it is despatched to Northbrook, Kaladar, and, eventually, the outer world.

Should he follow the alternate proceedure and carry that incoming mail with him to Denbigh and thence back to Bon Echo before depositing it in a box situate on the west side of the Highway, from which he would then also pick up outgoing mail, the modus operandi, it would seem to me, would still remain unsatisfactory. In either case, granting the use of a single box only, a lapse of twenty-four hours must ensue, whether the box be on the east side or the west side of the Highway, before urgent mail could possibly be answered. While such delays apparently mean little to the Canada Post Office, they can often assume importance in the affairs of a patron (or as Mr. Kierans, the Postmaster General, now prefers 'a customer') requiring recourse to the long distance telephone to affect communications which in a better ordered world would be handled by the postal authorities at a fraction of the cost.

While I have no wish to blame you, personally, for this sudden contretemps, I do feel constrained to call on you personally to come and help me out of what appears to be an impossible predicament and to do so before the threatened deadline of 11th August rolls around. Which shall be demolished? The east box or the west? The one on the left or the one on the right, going north or coming south?

Should I have failed in any way to state clearly my reaction to the situation arising from the application of your edict 13-3-100 CLOYNE R.R. No. 1, I will be glad to conduct any further correspondence with you in French.

Very truly yours,

Merrill Denison."

Over the years our friendly association with Lisa and Merrill continued and we visited them from time to time in their Simpson Street apartment in Montreal. At Bon Echo I remember happy summer evenings when we lingered over dinner on the Dollywood dining porch, watched the sunlight fade from the Rock and were entertained by Merrill's wit and wisdom. A frequent visitor in those days was Paul Clark, public relations vice president of the Aluminum Company of Canada, a good friend of Merrill's since they first met in the fifties at the Montreal Press Club.

Paul kindly "showed me the town" on one occasion when I was visiting the Denisons in Montreal. He took pity on a poor gal from the boondocks. I was impressed. At the Queen Elizabeth Hotel, ten or more couples were waiting to be seated in the dining room.

In the wink of an eye, Paul's quiet word to the maitre'd, no doubt accompanied by a sizeable tip, instantly brought a waiter to show us to a table. Later, we went to the movies, then on to a naughty floor show and finally to the Press Club where *Montreal Gazette* reporters were night-capping after putting the paper to bed, as they said. At three in the morning Merrill was still up, waiting for me to return.

Paul didn't drive a car, but I think was known to every taxi driver in the city. It was said that in the wee hours of the morning Paul didn't need to give his home address to the driver. When he planned a trip to Bon Echo he enlisted the services of a friendly young Scottish immigrant, Eddie Lang. With Paul as his mentor, Eddie began a career that took him to the top. It all started with a thorough understanding of his night-school text book, *Basic Accounting*.

My son, John Merrill, reminded me of the evening on the porch in Dollywood we were all sitting around the table in the candlelight after dinner when Lisa's beloved and pampered cat, Suzie, leapt up to seek attention from us all. Wandering from person to person between the candles, her long, fluffy tail caught fire. Eddie spat on his palm, grasped the base of Suzie's tail and quickly ran his hand up to the tip, putting out the fire. My young son admired Eddie's swift response.

During Merrill's last months in Montreal, Paul Clark was one of the very few who continued to visit the old man. They enjoyed their friendly arguments and their cribbage games. Paul was a faithful and understanding companion. In November, 1982, we heard from Eddie. He was now Edward J. Lang, President and Chief Executive Officer of Macdonald Inc., Toronto, (the tobacco people) and he wrote to tell us of Paul's death at the age of seventy-nine. "…I reflected on the good times we had had with Merrill, both of you and the three Mikes and all the mad visitors who had ever been to Mazinaw. Great times. Great memories." The three Mikes were Addinall, Huband and Schwager.

In 1971 there came a memorable and happy day for Merrill. In the foyer of the Hart House Theatre, University of Toronto, there is a plaque, unveiled on the 5th May, 1971, which is a permanent reminder of Merrill Denison, playwright. It marks the fiftieth anniversary of the day in 1921 when he wrote *Brothers-In-Arms*.

That May afternoon, at the Park Plaza Hotel, Merrill was excited, but he never would have admitted that. The weight of his seventy-eight years was evident. His breathing was laboured and he moved ever more slowly. He had grown a straggly beard, claiming it was too much trouble to shave. Nevertheless, he was bright and chipper, looking forward so much to the evening ahead. Like a teenager preparing for her first prom, he had Lisa check out his kilt, his shirt buttons, straighten his socks and smooth his hair.

Upon arrival at the theatre the Denisons were surrounded by friends, new and old. There were so many of them gathered around that I wasn't able to see Merrill unveil his plaque or hear what he said. The celebration dinner which followed at the Arts & Letters Club was attended by lots of famous Canadians. The master of ceremonies was old friend Mavor Moore, assisted by the Honourable Mr. Justice C. D. Stewart. Jack McClelland, Merrill's long-time publisher, proposed the toast. Newer friends included Tina and Mike Addinall. The highlight of the evening was the special performance of *Brothers-In-Arms*, produced by Robert Christie, well known in Canadian theatre, TV performances and father of Dinah Christie, a popular cabaret and TV personality.

The original 1921 theatre programme was reprinted, listing the two other Canadian plays. The first was *Pierre*, by Duncan Campbell Scott. Two of the five cast members had been Miss Muriel Goggin and Mr. Merrill Denison. The second play, *The Second Lie*, by Isabel Ecclestone MacKay, lists no less than Mr. Vincent Massey as a member of the cast. He eventually became the first Canadian-born Governor General. In that first production Merrill played Charlie Henderson. Charles Thompson, who had played Syd Marsh, James A. Cowan, the original stage manager and Colin Tait, technician, were all there to be with Merrill once again.

As he sat front row centre, I saw Merrill's lips moving with every word spoken on stage. The four actors were well-known Canadians, Ted Follows and Ed McNamara with Norma Clark and Gary Hall. It was a wonderful tribute to a great playwright. I regret that I never knew who master-minded that celebration. Whoever he was, (I don't suppose it was she) he must surely have understood the happiness and satisfaction Merrill experienced that day.

A departure from the norm was during the first months of 1973, when Merrill spent some weeks in residence alone at the Queen's Hotel on Brock Street, Kingston. Whether it was because he felt obliged to write in order to generate some income, or whether he was driven by his innate compulsion to write, is not clear. By then, apart from his old age pension, he no longer had a regular income and all his Mazinaw shoreline lots had been sold, so doubtless the bank accounts needed fattening.

In one small room he worked, slept and received an occasional guest. He was in Kingston because he needed access to his research notes in the Queen's University archives. We visited him there, a sad figure. Emphysema and a weak heart slowed him down. But though he was a tired old man, his determination to carry on was strong. His sharp wit and sense of humour had not deserted him. He'd rented an electric typewriter, to him a new-fangled piece of equipment that needed some getting used to.

He produced the rough copy of five chapters of *The Oldest Land*, a history of the Canadian Shield, progressing from Pre-Cambrian times through post-glacial lichens and mosses to the growth of plant and animal life, intending to go on to the story of man's desecration of Ontario's magnificent stands of marketable timber. He had been one of the first to mount the soap box to argue passionately against the clear-cutting of timber because he knew, first hand, the legacy of miserable poverty the lumber barons had left to the settlers, especially in the area of Bon Echo. In 1950 he had begun a similar work, *The Great North Woods*, which was written for the Department of Lands and Forests. It was never completed and never published. As was usual, Merrill gave me *The Oldest Land* chapters to type. That was the last manuscript I typed for him. He returned to Montreal and Lisa, unable to continue.

One more brief moment of recognition was the Hart House Theatre production of *Marsh Hay*, in March, 1974. Once again, friends rallied around the old man, now supporting himself with a walking stick. Though we were unable to be there, John Merrill enjoyed meeting some of the notables, including Jane Mallett, a well-known Canadian actress, authors W.0. Mitchell and Robertson Davies. Reviewers weren't impressed with the play. "Dialogue creaked as loudly as the revolving stage." It has been

Author, Mary Savigny, at Merrill's Memorial Service,
June 29, 1975.

Some of the congregation in the amphitheatre.

John J. Savigny at Story Lake, 1975.

suggested that audiences then just weren't interested in such a story of human misery, violence, teenage pregnancy and the sordid lives of a hopeless family in eastern Ontario's rural slum.

The climate had changed by 1996 when a professional production was staged by the Shaw Festival players at Niagara-on-the-Lake to uniformly rave reviews. Inches and inches of newspaper columns were devoted to Merrill and his work. His 1926 *Star Weekly* article, "Ontario's Ravished Wonderland," is quoted by Geoff Chapman in *The Toronto Star*:

> "We have been blinded to the tragic losses south of the Nipissing by the apparently illimitable resources to the north .... Our aversion to accept such facts that are unpleasant to us and pleasant opiates of romantic fiction which soothe us with lovely stories of the 'great open spaces' where men are men and every woman is a lady and often a flower, have made it easy for us to evade any responsibility for the poor human beings scratching a living among the barren hills to which they are chained through poverty as actually as if manacles held them to the rocks .... The fact that the backwoods form a vast rural slum .... to blame the settler is to show a complete ignorance of those condition."

Two paintings of Bon Echo Rock by
Eric Aldwinckle done in 1960.

Throughout 1974 Merrill's health continued to decline. The need for cash was an ever-present problem. He tried to sell the Alex Jackson original Bon Echo poster to the National Gallery. "(It) should command a goodly price although it does nothing to enhance the old master's high repute." That summer was his last at Bon Echo.

At a party across the lake, at Nadine Brumell's cottage, he became faint and lapsed into semi-consciousness. Taken speedily by boat to the marina, he was transported by ambulance to Belleville General Hospital. When he was a little stronger, Lisa explored the possibility of getting him settled into a nursing home in Belleville, however they returned to Montreal and a difficult winter when a series of mild strokes hospitalized him on several occasions. Lisa's letter to us of the 23rd April, 1975, says in part:

> "As you have probably heard, I have been to California, and bought a house. It is in Solana Beach, 5 miles from Del Mar and the Andrews [Lisa's son and family] and 9 miles from the U.S. Army Veterans' Hospital in La Jolla, where I hope Merrill will be comfortable, cared for and content.
>
> Jeanette Casenave will fly with him to California, and then visit her parents near Pasadena. I will be at Bon Echo soon after their exodus. And then return to Montreal to wind up, pack up and decamp as soon as possible. Moving date is set for June 27th."

Merrill was taken to the veterans' hospital early in May and there, among strangers, he suffered a fatal stroke on the 12th June, 1975, eleven days before his eighty-second birthday. Lisa arranged a memorial service in McGill Chapel, Divinity Hall, Montreal, on the 17th, before leaving for California, and on Sunday, the 29th June, 1975, a memorial service was held in the amphitheatre at Bon Echo. Roy Evans, the park chaplain, conducted the service.

As I sat at the organ waiting for the service to begin, a Mazinaw cottager approached and demanded to know why a religious service was being held to honour a man who had declared himself a disbeliever. I told him we were thanking God for the life of Merrill Denison, that we were thankful for having known him. The amphitheatre was full. The flags were flown at half-staff.

Representatives of the Department of Lands and Forests and local politicians paid tribute to the memory of the man whose vision, determination and generosity had made Bon Echo Provincial Park a reality. Roy Evans, having read the story of Merrill's early brush with organized religion, said that if the young Merrill that day in Sunday School had been introduced to the gentle and loving Son rather than hearing the story of a demanding Father, perhaps he might have become a Christian.

Merrill had lived a long, complicated and useful life. It is gratifying to know that at least one of his plays has finally received the recognition it deserves. His unique genius as a Canadian historian is generally unremarked. His ability to gather together the dry statistics, board meeting minutes and financial statements of a corporation to produce an interesting, readable book was remarkable. He understood that personalities, not statistics, made the corporate wheels turn and so shape the course of a nation. It had been necessary, as Merrill said, for him to become, in turn, a farm machinery mechanic, brewer, distiller, auto mechanic, banker and politician-cum-electrical-hydraulic engineer.

In response to an article in *The Kingston Whig-Standard* in 1992 by Peter Christie, who had reviewed a Bon Echo exhibition at Queen's University, and had reported that Merrill Denison sold his property to the province, John Savigny wrote:

> "Merrill Denison did not sell the Bon Echo property, as stated in the article. He gave it to the Province of Ontario 'for all the people.'
>
> This gift would have been exceedingly generous had it been made by a wealthy industrialist with vast holdings. It is the more remarkable and to be appreciated because Merrill Denison was a relatively poor man."

The bald mountains and barren slopes of the backwoods denuded by forest fires and greedy lumber barons, which Merrill, his mother and Muriel knew, have become green again. Nature healed the wounds. Now the people of the area live comfortable lives and visitors to Bon Echo Provincial Park enjoy a rejuvenated land and can only read about and imagine the scenes of long ago. At Bon Echo, the place he loved best, Merrill Denison will be remembered.

Endnotes

1   Merrill Denison, *The Barley and the Stream. The Molson Story*. McClelland & Stewart Toronto, 1955, p.39.

2   Letters from Merrill Denison to Mary Savigny, January 1954.

3   Ibid, November, 1953.

4   Ibid

5   Letter from Conway Turton to Mary Savigny, February, 1954

6   Letter from Merrill Denison to Mary Savigny, February, 1954

7   Foreword, *The Barley and the Stream*. McClelland & Stewart, 1955.

8   Bon Echo Inn Brochure, circa 1930.

9   Ibid

10 Letter from B.J. Holloway to John and Mary Savigny, 24th August, 1954.

11 Ibid

12 "Crusts and Crumbs" was a regular column written for *The Toronto Sunday World* by Albert Ernest Stafford, c. 1916.

13 Dr. Richard Maurice Bucke, *Cosmic Consciousness*. Innes & Sons, Philadelphia. 1st edition 1901. Latest edition 1993.

Publisher's Note

The information and opinions contained within this publication are those of the author, Mary Savigny. Both the copyright holder and the publisher, Natural Heritage/Natural History Inc., will be pleased to correct any erroneous information in future editions.

Selected Works of Merrill Denison

Books

The Unheroic North. Four plays; McLelland & Stewart, 1923

Boobs in the Woods. Sixteen sketches by one of them. Graphic Publishers, 1927

By Guess and By God. With W.G. Carr. The story of British Submarines in the War (WW1). Doubleday, Doran & Company, 1930.

Henry Hudson and Other Plays. The Ryerson Press, 1931

Our Great Ones. With Jack McLaren. A Folio of Linocuts; The Ryerson Press, 1932

Advancing America. (information not available)

Niagara's Pioneers. The Niagara Falls Power Company (no date available)

The U.S. vs Susan B. Anthony. A one-act play for young people dealing with freedom and democracy; Dramatists Play Service Inc., New York City, 1941

Canada, Our Dominion Neighbor. Foreign Policy Assocation Inc., New York City, 1944

Klondike Mike: An Alaskan Odyssey. William Morrow & Co., 1943

Bristles and Brushes. A Footnote to the Story of American War Production (WW2); Dodd, Mead & Company, 1949

Harvest Triumphant. The Story of Massey-Harris. McLelland & Stewart, 1948

The Barley and the Stream. The Molson Story. McLelland & Stewart, 1955

The Power to Go. The Story of the Automobile Industry. Doubleday & Company Inc., 1956

The People's Power. The History of Ontario Hydro. McLelland & Stewart, 1960

Canada's First Bank. A History of the Bank of Montreal. McLelland & Stewart, Volume I, 1966, Volume II, 1967

Unpublished Book Manuscripts

An Old Sheep Drinks Deep. Merrill's boyhood in Toronto c1920

The Great North Woods. Incomplete. 1950

The Oldest Land. Incomplete. 1973

Radio Drama

Jack and Jill. The Romance of Canada Series.

Maple Centre. Great Moments in History.

Pickwick Papers. Women of America and other documentaries.

Magazines

Star Weekly. Ladies' Home Journal.
MacLeans. New Yorker.
Reader's Digest. Strand.
Canadian Bookman. Harper's and many articles in other periodicals.

Muriel Denison and the Susannah Books

Susannah: A Little Girl With the Mounties. 1st printing, 1936;
    12th printing, 1950.
Susannah of the Yukon. 1st printing, 1937; 7th printing, 1959.
Susannah at Boarding School. 1st printing, 1938
Susannah Rides Again. 1st printing, 1940.
All books published by Dodd, Mead & Co.

Milestones

1893 Born in Detroit, Michigan

1901 First visit to Lake Mazinaw

1910 His mother, Flora MacDonald Denison, buys Bon Echo

1916 Service in France with the U.S. Ambulance Corps

1917 Service in France with the U.S. Army

1921 Writes *Brothers-In-Arms*

1921 His mother dies

1926 Marries Jessie Muriel Goggin

1929 Bankruptcy of Bon Echo Inn Limited

1930 Writes first radio drama for NBC in New York City

1948 First corporate history, *Harvest Triumphant*, published

1954 Muriel, his first wife, dies

1957 Marries Elizabeth Robert Andrews

1959 Bon Echo deeded to Her Majesty the Queen

1965 Bon Echo plaque unveiled, a gift to the People of Ontario

1971 Hart House Theatre plaque unveiled and 50th anniversary
    production of *Brothers-In-Arms*

1975 Dies in La Jolla, California

Visual Credits

Cover Credit: Painting by Arthur Lismer. Courtesy of Mrs. Marjorie Lismer Bridges and the Mendel Gallery, Saskatoon.

Inside front cover: Upper, Courtesy of Alice Beswick. Middle, From "Douglas Library Notes", Courtesy of Queen's University Archives. Lower, Courtesy of Queen's University Archives.

Inside back cover: Upper, Photo by Janet Birnie. Lower, Courtesy of Shaw Festival Theatre.

Page i: Frank (Franz) Johnston, Courtesy of Mrs. Wenawae Stevenson: Collection of the author.

Page ii: Portrait by Nakash.

Page iv: Collection of the author.

Page vi: Collection of the author.

Page xi: Collection of the author.

Page xii Lower: Courtesy of Department of Lands and Forests.

Page xiii Upper: Courtesy of Department of Lands and Forests. Lower: Collection of the author.

Page xiv Upper left and right: Collection of the author. Lower: left and right: Courtesy of Robert C. Baron, Fulcrum Publishing, Colorado.

Page 2. Collection of the author.

Page 4. Collection of the author.

Page 7. Collection of the author.

Page 12. Courtesy of Queen's University Archives.

Page 14. Courtesy of Friends of Bon Echo Park.

Page 15. Collection of the author.

Page 19. Upper left: Collection of the author, courtesy of Mrs. Wenawae Stevenson. Upper right: Collection of the author. Lower left: Collection of the author, courtesy of Dr. Naomi Jackson Groves.

Page 20 – 21. Collection of the author.

Page 22. Left: Collection of the author. Right: Painting of M. Denison by Frank (Franz) Johnston, courtesy of Mrs. Wenawae Stevenson.

Page 26. Photography by John Milne, Toronto, Queen's University Archives.

Page 29. *The Toronto Star Weekly*, 1930

Page 31. Collection of the author.

Page 34. Collection of the author.

Page 39. Collection of the author.

Page 41. Collection of the author.

Page 46 Left and right: Courtesy of Queen's University Archives.

Page 51. Collection of the author.

Page 52 Upper: Courtesy of Queen's University Library, Lower: Courtesy of Alice Beswick.

Page 53. Upper and lower: Courtesy of Alice Beswick.

Page 58. Collection of the author.

Page 59. Collection of the author.

Page 60. Courtesy of Queen's University Archives.

Page 67. Photo by Nat Turofsky, courtesy of Queen's University Archives.

Page 70. Photo by Nat Turofsky, courtesy of Queen's University Archives.

Page 71. Photos by Nat Turofsky, courtesy of Queen's University Archives.

Page 76. Collection of the author.

Page 85. Collection of the author.

Page 87. Collection of the author.

Page 90. Collection of the author.

Page 94. Photo by Lisa Denison. Collection of the author.

Page 97. Courtesy of The Department of Lands and Forests.

Page 99. Courtesy of Tony Brumell, Kamloops, B.C.

Page 100. Courtesy of Terry Van Kempen, Mazinaw Lake.

Page 111. Collection of the author.

Page 112. Collection of the author.

Page 113 Collection of the author. Both visuals courtesy of the Aldwinckle family.

Page 130. Collection of the author.

Index

About the Author

MARY SAVIGNY was born Mary Kirby in Sheffield, Yorkshire, England, in 1923. At the age of thirteen, unable to pursue an education in fine art, she found employment as a junior shorthand-typist at a small tool-steel firm in Sheffield. At sixteen, she progressed to a mine surveyor's office where she was the sole employee. In the evenings, when the German air blitz would allow, she typed manuscripts for Sir Osbert Sitwell and his sister, Dame Edith Sitwell.

In 1942 she joined the RAF as an operations room plotter, first at RAF Hornchurch, a Spitfire fighter station in Essex, and in 1943 at the Air-Sea Rescue control room at RAF Swingate, Dover. There she met John, an RCAF radar mechanic, her future husband. After two more years of war and a year in Toronto they moved to Northbrook, Ontario, where she later met Merrill Denison.

While a partner in Savigny Real Estate Limited, she studied art at the North Addington Education Centre evening classes under Fred Schonberger. In 1977 she achieved her early ambition to study art by attending the fine art course at St. Lawrence College in Kingston. In 1979 she was appointed a governor of Loyalist College, Belleville, and was a member of the print journalism committee.

In 1987 she and her husband retired to Kingston. They have three children; Janet Birnie of Oakville, Ontario; David of Cloyne, Ontario; and John Merrill of Fenwick, Ontario. *Bon Echo: The Denison Years* is her first book.